The Successful President

"BuzzWords" on Leadership

by
Kenneth A. Shaw

Foreword by
Donna E. Shalala

AMERICAN COUNCIL ON EDUCATION ★
ORYX PRESS ★
Series on Higher Education
1999

The rare Arabian Oryx is believed to have inspired the myth of the unicorn. This desert antelope became virtually extinct in the early 1960s. At that time, several groups of international conservationists arranged to have nine animals sent to the Phoenix Zoo to be the nucleus of a captive breeding herd. Today, the Oryx population is over 1,000, and over 500 have been returned to the Middle East.

© 1999 by The American Council on Education and The Oryx Press
4041 North Central at Indian School Road
Phoenix, Arizona 85012-3397

Published simultaneously in Canada
Printed and bound in the United States of America

∞ The paper used in this publication meets the minimum requirements of American National Standard for Information Science—Permanence of Paper for Printed Library Materials, ANSI Z39.48, 1984.

Library of Congress Cataloging-in-Publication Data

Shaw, Kenneth A.
 The successful President : "buzzwords" on leadership / by
Kenneth A. Shaw.
   p. cm. — (American Council on Education/Oryx Press series on
higher education)
  Includes bibliographical references and index.
  ISBN 1-57356-300-5 (alk. paper)
  1. Universities and colleges—United States—Administration.
2. College presidents—United States. 3. Educational leadership
—United States. I. Title. II. Series.
LB2341.S46   1999
378.1'01—dc21   99-12926
                                                                          CIP

To academic leaders, past and present,
who have created the world's best system of higher education.

To leaders of the next millennium,
who hold our future in their hands.

CONTENTS

FOREWORD

by Donna E. Shalala

K enneth "Buzz" Shaw is one of the most experienced and knowledgeable leaders in higher education. He also is a great teacher and
coach of higher education's new generation of administrators. I
should know: In the late 1980s and early 1990s, I had a chance to learn
from him. As president of the University of Wisconsin System, he was
instrumental in recruiting me to be chancellor of the University of Wisconsin–Madison.

While Shaw uses his current institution, Syracuse University (my alma
mater), as a case study, his experience in public higher education in Illinois
and Wisconsin makes his ideas equally applicable to administrators in
public colleges and universities, and at both small and large institutions.
Indeed, as a manager now of a large, complex, federal agency, I have
learned a number of important lessons from this book. I wish this classic
had been available during my first university presidency!

Shaw begins with a personal account of leading Syracuse through the
process of restructuring in response to the harsh economic climate of the
early 1990s. He promoted the university's restructuring as positive change
by using it as an opportunity to involve the community in decision making,
to improve the quality of work throughout the university, to renew the
institution's values and mission, and to validate the strength of the university by showing it the faith and loyalty it deserved. The result was a greater
sense of hope on campus, students who were more satisfied and performed
better, and national attention from other higher education institutions
whose leaders have emulated Syracuse's success.

In this insightful book, Shaw shares his definition of leadership as persuasion and example balanced with the institution's vision and goals, and he analyzes leadership traits such as good communication skills, the ability to adapt to change, and the capacity to manage effectively. Added to these are interpersonal competencies in areas such as conflict resolution, the effective use of power, and motivating others.

Shaw also describes the constituencies with which a leader must work in an institution—including faculty, students, board members, alumni, and government officials. As a former star basketball player, Shaw understands teamwork as a critical element for the success of any complex organization. Thus, he emphasizes the importance of group skills, defining the leader's role as seeking consensus, fostering creativity, and encouraging participation.

The best advice, from my point of view, is found in the chapter on crisis management. Shaw contends that positive change *can* be achieved—through openness, reassurance, preparation, support, and reward. Good leaders have a plan and a process. Delegating authority and responsibility, and including everyone in the decision-making process, will ensure a smoother transition. He also advocates the novel approach of treating a crisis in the university as a loss, and dealing with the resulting "organizational grief" as a necessary step on the path to productive restructuring.

Shaw addresses the public side of leadership, too. He discusses the responsibility of the president as spokesperson and gives examples of how to remain calm under pressure. He lists practical tips for public speaking, fund raising, and dealing with the press during ceremonial occasions, social gatherings, town-gown relations, and personal appearances in the community.

All in all, this is an extraordinarily pragmatic, insightful, motivating book, written by a colleague in the middle of his leadership career—not at the end. Shaw helps both students and practitioners of academic management and leadership understand the need to be visible and principled and nimble.

Every new president and chancellor should have this book on their desk. It will be well-worn by the end of their first year.

PREFACE

W hile the subject of leadership is much discussed these days, the essence of the process remains elusive. This is true in spite of the national dismay about leaders, in spite of the microscopic examination of leaders by the press and others, and in spite of the growing need for more and more people who can lead well, at least at some point in their lives and probably many times throughout their adulthood.

I don't mean to imply that no one is giving leadership serious study. Indeed, our libraries are full of excellent texts on the topic. Widely respected scholars have devoted decades to the study. Some have staked their careers on this study—John Gardner the best known of all. Others have carved out a niche in areas like health care, business and industry, and, of course, higher education.

I highly recommend the work of Robert Birnbaum, James MacGregor Burns, Estela Bensimon, and James L. Fisher. Each author draws on strong theoretical frameworks and creates a sound basis for our understanding of the deeper meaning of leadership and the motivations and pitfalls experienced by all kinds of leaders. As a student of leadership myself, I am indebted to these and other writers in the field. I have read their work with great interest, and I suggest you do so, too, as time allows.

But this book offers a practical approach to leading. I draw on my own studentship in the field plus more than 20 years' experience as a leader in higher education. As a blend of book learning and more than a few hard knocks, this isn't a theoretical tome nor is it a coffee-table showpiece. It's not a hand-holding exercise. Your leadership experience will be uniquely your own. Nevertheless, the tools described in these pages have proved useful to me and many of my colleagues.

Knowing that my readers are busy people, I have covered each topic so that it can be read and digested in one sitting. However, since there is a logic to the order in which topics are presented, I suggest each chapter be read in sequence. I invite readers to underline, dog-ear, and otherwise personalize their copies and refer to them from time to time as needed. (Did I mention that leading is stressful? Trust me when I say that people who lead need all the help they can get. That's really what this book is for.)

One caveat: This is not a cookbook approach to leading. If you hope to find a step-by-step recipe of specific traits or activities that will result in a palatable leader, this book will disappoint you. I don't believe it is possible to write a prescription for leadership. The best I can offer—or any student of the subject can offer—are insights and guidelines to help make the process of leading more effective and more rewarding.

Let's face it: leading is often a lonely and sometimes thankless undertaking. Some scholars maintain it doesn't even make a difference, given modern organizational and social constraints. Others believe that leaders are born, not made, and no amount of education can turn a non-leader into a leader.

Clearly, I don't hold those positions. If you do, put down this book; reading more will only frustrate you. Naturally there are constraints to leading that didn't exist in earlier decades. The rigid, bureaucratic organization with the benevolent despot at the top has given way to a far more horizontal structure with many teams and many leaders. Leading today requires far more group and interpersonal savvy than before. And I believe that those and other skills can be learned and practiced.

I don't look at this important subject wearing rose-colored glasses. I know that most organizations change very slowly. I also know they must change or be left behind. While experienced leaders know they can make incremental moves in the right direction if they are patient, observant, and courageous, it is also true that sometimes major, thrilling, and soul-satisfying breakthroughs can and do happen. A transforming leader is comfortable with both the incremental and the blockbuster paces.

Finally, this book will concentrate on leading in higher education. While much of what I write can be used in other organizations and institutions, I simply don't have the experience necessary to comment intelligently on leading in other arenas. I know what has worked for me in the colleges and universities I have served.

This is not, however, a prescription for what might ail higher education in general. That's another kind of book—one that is important and the subject of which many other writers are tackling. You and I know that change is the only constant on college campuses, and what works today will be outmoded in a very short time. It's also true that what might work at one kind of university won't make sense at another. Leaders must keep abreast of issues that affect their particular institutions now and in the future. But most important, they must know how to lead.

This book offers a set of understandings that will stand the test of time. These are tools that can be applied in virtually any situation where change, an institution, and stakeholders come together.

The chapters are organized as follows: chapter 1 is a story of transformation at Syracuse University; chapter 2 includes various definitions of leadership; chapter 3 focuses on interpersonal competencies such as conflict resolution, effective use of power, and motivating others; chapter 4 concentrates on working in and with groups; chapter 5 is about leading an institution through crisis and toward positive change; chapter 6 covers the public side of leadership; chapter 7 includes empirical observations; and chapter 8 offers a handy summary plus a section on future selection and training of academic leaders.

ACKNOWLEDGMENTS

T here are many people to credit for shaping this book. They are my friends and colleagues of many years, individuals who have applauded my successes, helped me make decisions, and, most important, pointed out where I've gone wrong.

My professors at Illinois State University, the University of Illinois, and Purdue University encouraged me to expect more of myself, especially when I felt confident I'd done all I could. In particular, I credit Lee Isaacson, my major professor at Purdue, who allowed me the flexibility of reviewing much of the literature on leadership as part of my studies.

I thank my mentors—Bob Bone, Sam Braden, Jim Fisher, and Dick Hulet—for their unflagging inspiration and for setting the bar higher at each step along the way. I am grateful to the many colleagues at Towson State, Southern Illinois University, the University of Wisconsin System, and Syracuse University whose wisdom and experience increased my own many times over.

And I thank those who have read this text and offered suggestions for its improvement as it has taken shape. Kathryn Lee, my editorial assistant, read, edited, reread, and discussed these words with me many times and cared very much that they conveyed my thoughts on this topic. Mary Ann Shaw, my wife and best friend, has been a strong source of support for me as my own leadership has evolved. It was her insistence that I share my views on leadership that led to this book.

CHAPTER 1

A Story

*The world is moving so fast these days that the man who says it can't
be done is generally interrupted by someone doing it.*
—Elbert Hubbard

'm going to tell you a story about Syracuse University. There is no
ending, happy or otherwise, since it is an institution in progress. But this
is still a happy story (you didn't really think I would begin this with a
dismal failure, did you?).

What follows is my perspective, as president, on the process of restructuring that Syracuse began in 1991 and continues today. It has involved
literally thousands of people—faculty, staff, students, alumni, trustees, and
others—who came forward to exert leadership at a critical juncture in the
university's history. The pride they feel in their accomplishments is well
justified.

The institution is not without challenges, however. (As I write, we are
recovering from a week-long strike by our service workers' union, which
was followed by a storm packing 75-mile-an-hour winds that downed trees
and electrical wires all over the city. I've been credited with both.) In spite
of this, though, we are clearly in a stronger position to accomplish our
mission than we were eight years ago.

After the story is told, I move into the heart of this book—my advice on
improving your leadership skills.

But first...

THE TALE BEGINS

The setting is Syracuse University (SU), a mid-sized, private research institution located in the northeast United States. For more than a century, this institution had slowly but surely built its reputation to a national level. While it had the requisite ivy covering on fine old buildings, it was also a place where change had happened, sometimes rapidly. For example, it was one of the universities that made itself fully available to GIs returning from World War II. The resulting surge in enrollment was the catalyst for a great period of growth not only in physical size but in the estimation of those who mattered—scholars, funding agencies, alumni, and prospective students.

This steady upward climb lasted more than 35 years. By the 1980s Syracuse was on a roll. Undergraduate enrollment stood at 12,000 students, just 15 percent of its tuition income was allocated for institutional financial aid, and between $10 and $15 million a year was tucked away into a reserve fund.

And then a new reality hit. By the end of the 1980s, the predicted demographic shift in the numbers of college-going 18-year-olds made its presence known. This 20 percent decrease in the applicant pool was coupled with an economy that seemed to be built on sand.

Enrollment dropped and many more students required financial aid. In an increasingly competitive market, the latter became an essential marketing tool, especially for recruiting students of exceptional merit.

By 1990, SU projected an annual deficit of approximately $40 million if no actions were taken.

Switching Leaders in Midstream

There was another major change in the works. Syracuse University's leader, Chancellor Melvin A. Eggers, was ready to retire. And that was where I came in. I had enjoyed many years in state higher education systems, the last of which was in Wisconsin where I served as system president. I was intrigued and challenged by an opportunity in the private sector, and in 1991 I accepted SU's chancellorship.

I knew that at Syracuse two fronts had to be addressed quickly for a chance of success. The fiscal situation needed to be resolved with a solid plan, of course. But the institutional community also needed to be brought together to work in new and more productive ways. And to give both areas the best possible chance, the faculty, staff, students, alumni, trustees, and others had to sign on to their common mission and vision with far greater conviction than before.

To speed up the process, well before I officially arrived on campus, I convened representative groups to talk with them about the issues they felt were most important. They were to supply me with volumes of information. From these sessions, I hoped to identify a consensus on the top five or more issues with which this institution would have to deal in the near future or face even more serious problems.

The summer prior to my arrival was busier than most that SU's campus had experienced in recent memory. People were working side by side with others they may not have known, or, in some cases, actively disliked. Spurred by a new sense of urgency, these groups were remarkably productive. One committee in particular dealt with the university's projected budget challenges. It had been appointed by Mel Eggers as his parting contribution to the institution he had so ably led. He had given them a mandate to define all the parameters of the budgetary challenge and to begin the process of suggesting solutions. Their findings were made available to me when I took office in mid-August.

On Arrival

Still, once I got to campus, I found people entering the grieving process in response to the budgetary challenge. Some suggested that the institution just needed to be more cost-effective. For others, the answer was closing a program. The trouble was that each had in mind a different area to be axed (never her or his own, naturally). Others said, "Make the admissions people go out and get more students," leaving unspoken the assumption that standards would likely drop. Still others wanted to batten down the hatches and ride out the storm until the predicted upturn in the 18-year-old population occurred.

A small but vocal number found ways to get close to me to proclaim that morale was at an all-time low. For them, the answer was crystal clear: Fire _____! The blank was filled in differently depending on who was speaking, but all cherished a firm belief that if only so-and-so were dismissed, all would be well. It was tempting to listen to the catalog of sins that those who favored the personnel problem theory were only too eager to share.

Ad hominem attacks, though, were not what was needed at this time. They were a form of denial, just like the finger pointing and wishful thinking in which others were engaging.

I chose to accept the grieving process and also to use every opportunity to reinforce the need to move quickly toward solutions, even as I validated the strength of this university and the faith and loyalty it deserved. So, while budget work dominated the ensuing months, there were many occasions to articulate and repeat the mission, vision, and core values of the institution.

VALUES, MISSION, AND VISION

In the early stages of restructuring, the internal and larger communities were confused and frightened. It was important for them to remember that the institution had five strong core values—quality, caring, innovation, diversity, and service. These, as much as the ledger sheets, would guide the process of making financial sacrifices.

Accordingly, the core values were reinforced through speeches, reports, meetings, and other university community events. In this way, the groundwork was laid for the hard work that was to come. The bottom line was that budget decisions would be judged by how they preserved the values.

In time the institution's mission was recast into a statement about the responsibility of faculty, students, and staff to promote learning through teaching, research, scholarship, creative accomplishment, and service. From that came the vision to become the nation's leading student-centered research institution.

Pandora's Box

At the same time, an accurate and complete picture of the university's financial situation was shared with the community openly and widely. Largely by means of the campus newspaper, and reinforced through speeches and meetings, the fiscal strengths and weaknesses of each of the schools and colleges and the administrative units were aired.

In certain cases, people learned for the first time that some units were shouldering the financial burden disproportionately, while others depended on the largesse of the institution for as much as 80 percent of their operating funds. Even the legendary reserve fund, once shrouded in secrecy and therefore widely assumed to be on a par with King Solomon's mines, was opened for view. And a team of consultants was hired to assess the administrative units to ferret out bloat.

A preliminary plan, developed by the vice chancellor, was published, in which guidelines for restructuring the institution were suggested. With this information available, the community was asked to make suggestions and proposals that would be in keeping with the mission, vision, and values. The response was heartening. The university senate, composed largely of faculty representatives, made more than 100 policy recommendations (90 percent of which were approved). More than 150 community members sent thoughtful responses and advice.

In very short order—less than six months after I took office—the full restructuring report was ready. It was released as an insert in the campus newspaper following a major address to the community on the same day. The report revealed that administrative units were cut disproportionately in comparison to academic units. The exceptions were areas such as counseling and public safety, clearly key areas for student welfare and well-being. Within the academic units, cuts were made strategically according, in part, to a quality-centrality-demand metric. Thus one unit was given a budget add-on of nearly $1 million, while another dealt with cuts nearing 50 percent. All the schools and colleges were then left to the hard work of making their assigned cuts so that the unique ways in which they embodied the values, mission, and vision of the institution would be preserved.

The human restructuring costs were never hidden. Supported resignations, layoffs, and vacancies left unfilled were hard facts of life. Accordingly the human resources function at the university received some additional financial support for counseling and advising those who were let go. Supervisors across campus were advised to exercise heightened sensitivity, not only to those who were laid off but also to those who stayed on to feel the loss of their colleagues and to shoulder the extra work that came with a smaller staff. Thus, while the work of the university went on, the grieving process was given due respect.

33 Initiatives

As tough as this time was for the university, it was also an excellent opportunity to target areas of strength and to work toward improving them. The institution was renewing itself as well as experiencing some fiscal pain. Therefore, along with the messages about budget cuts came a detailed plan for positive change known as the 33 initiatives.

While they ranged from a quality improvement plan for the administrative areas to a classroom-focused effort for new students, the overarching purpose was to give the community opportunities to participate fully in serving their institution's mission and vision. Of course there was cynicism.

People who make their living by thinking and analyzing almost never take things at face value. Thus, the plan was given muscle with a $2 million fund for innovation, the dedication of financial and human resource support for a new quality improvement initiative, and a continuing update on the progress of the initiatives as they were implemented, achieved, and adapted to meet changing needs.

STAYING THE COURSE

Naturally there were bumps in the road. From the beginning, some members of the community refused to give the plan their full endorsement. Some were immediately enthusiastic. The great majority in the middle, however, wanted to be supportive but were unsure of what was going to happen next.

I continually revisited the plan at meetings, in speeches, and in written communication. I also reminded everyone that predicting the future was extremely difficult, given the fluid nature of higher education at the century's end. I noted many times that the plan would have to be adapted over time and asked advice and counsel on budget matters frequently. By keeping these issues out in front, I was informing the community that challenges weren't going to go away and that there were no easy answers. Terms like *trade-off*, *strategic plan*, and *priorities* became common currency.

I also made certain that successes were publicly acknowledged and praised. An all-out effort to streamline the bursar's operation virtually eliminated the long lines of unhappy students that had always signaled the beginning of a new semester. A revamped method to maintain the physical infrastructure cut costs and created better relations between building occupants and the people who cleaned and repaired them. These victories and many others became news stories and anecdotes in presidential communication.

More and more community members came on board, willing to give this plan an honest try. Successes, then, led to still more. Even the failures became easier to take in the new "we're all in this together" atmosphere.

Nevertheless, undergraduate enrollment did drop by nearly 2,000 (which proved to be a blessing later on). And it was necessary to provide more financial aid than predicted to attract the caliber of students the university desired.

A mid-course cut of $6 million on top of the previous cuts was implemented. Like the first set of budget cuts, these held the core educational functions harmless as much as possible. The schools and colleges, for example, experienced a 2 percent cut compared to a nearly 4 percent cut on the administrative side. Some initiatives such as the honors program, the college learning skills program, and the future professoriate program received incentive funds.

This meant a further reduction in numbers of staff, bringing totals to nearly 200 fewer faculty members (all through supported resignations or retirement) and more than 400 fewer staff members (a third through attrition).

A WORK IN PROGRESS

Today Syracuse University operates quite differently than it had. It has renewed itself and in the process it has grieved, let go of some of its past, come to terms with a new reality, and become better.

The proof is in a greater sense of hope on campus. Caring about the quality of one's work has been heightened. The willingness to embrace change has grown significantly, as has impatience as improvements demonstrate that things can get better.

There is harder evidence. National polls have ranked SU consistently higher in recent years. National awards have highlighted the changes underway. National attention, especially from other higher education institutions, has focused on emulating this university's successes.

Best of all, though, has been the growth in satisfaction registered by current students. Greater numbers of them persist through graduation. Many more students strongly encourage others to apply for admission. This, in turn, has led to an increase in applications and admissions in recent years combined with rising test scores and high school class rankings.

No one could be more pleased with these positive signs than the leadership of this institution. Though the issues faced were highly complex, they were addressed with speed and certainty. Reduced to simple terms, the plan went like this:

- First, identify and reinforce core institutional values
- Use those values as a backdrop for decision making
- Share all relevant financial information with the campus community
- Involve the community not only in the grieving process as colleagues are let go and as organizational change occurs, but also in the decision-making process
- Use the opportunity as a time of renewal and quality improvement, as well as fiscal responsibility

That's one story. There are many more. Some I have experienced personally; others have been relayed to me by colleagues and friends. I include them as illustrations of some very important leadership principles and skills.

CHAPTER 2

Leadership Defined

The difference between leaders and managers is that managers do things right and leaders do the right things.

—Warren Bennis

As I mentioned in the preface, there are a number of great books on the theory of leadership. The theories espoused (and disputed) include the trait theory, the social exchange theory, the behavior theory, the contingency theory, the cultural/symbolic theory, and the cognitive theory. Students of social organization will recognize these and the hierarchy of sophistication in which they fit. I, for one, believe that all these theories have merit and each can be found in any leadership tenure of any duration.

But this, as you recall, is not a theoretical exercise. It is a practical application of my knowledge, study, and observations to the tasks of leading a higher education institution.

Before I begin, I want you to know how I define leadership. Here I borrow from John Gardner, who says that leading is a process of persuasion and example by which one person induces others to take action.[1] The direction of that action will be in accord with the leader's purposes.

For Gardner the definition hangs on the words *persuasion, example,* and *action,* particularly *group action.* I add a modification: leading is a process of persuasion and example by which one person induces others to take action in accordance with the leader's purposes and the institution's mission, vision, and values. This isn't a treatise on the pros and cons of top-down versus democratic leadership. Nevertheless, I don't believe any leader can

9

be successful without aligning his or her purposes with those of the institution and the people it serves and is served by. In fact, I'll go so far as to say that any leader who ignores values, vision, and people is doomed to a tenure of frustration and failure.

In my view, frustration and a healthy portion of failure are already built into leadership. Leading is a lonely business. Even on a good day, there will be stress. After all, good leadership isn't necessary when everything is running smoothly. Good leadership is needed when there are problems, and good leaders recognize that much of the time they will deal with the negatives and let the positives take care of themselves. Why add to the stress by moving away from the direction the institution already wants and needs to go? Occasionally, there needs to be a significant course correction, but usually not.

Now to the heart of the matter—what leaders do.

THE TASKS OF LEADERSHIP

Envisioning and Affirming Goals and Values

An institution's various constituencies generally and out of necessity concentrate on their particular needs and functions. Students, for example, are busy studying, forming friendships, and having fun, not necessarily in that order. Faculty members are concerned with their courses and scholarship. But the leader is charged with defining the overall vision and guarding the institution's core values. This is the view from the rooftop that others, too busy meeting responsibilities, miss.

One college president was labeled a good leader because she "pointed us in the right direction." Another president identified his institution's core values as quality, caring, diversity, innovation, and service. These were not new to the university; rather, they needed emphasis and repetition so that the budgetary and other challenges could be met without sacrificing what made that institution unique.

Articulating Goals and Values

Identified goals and values are all well and good, but even the clearest and most inspirational of these will die on the vine if they are not communicated effectively and often. The leader's job is to make certain that these messages are carried by every means available. That includes formal channels such as the institution's own publications and video presentations. Just as important are the messages the leader conveys at ceremonial occasions, social gatherings, and personal appearances in the community. These can and ought to be occasions to educate others about the essence of the college or university and to place recent decisions in that context.

Leaders need not fear overstressing the goals and values. One of my teachers in elementary school stressed that repetition was the key to learning—and she said that often! Nothing I've observed in the years since has proved her wrong.

Implementing Goals and Values

Identification and articulation must lead to implementation—and as quickly as possible, especially in times of challenge. While not every goal can be achieved quickly, some clear evidence of success will serve as a galvanizing force for the campus community and a reassurance that the institution is headed in the right direction. For the leader, this means motivating people to move in directions consonant with the core values and with the stated goals. I'll have more on this important task later, but suffice it to say now that motivating requires good communication skills, an atmosphere of trust, and an ability to manage effectively.

To implement goals and values, leaders need to be managers, not perfect managers, but good-enough managers. Good-enough managers know how to get things done and done right.

Serving as the Keeper of the Institution's Goals and Values

Leaders are the institution's conscience. Often this role requires a willingness to ask hard questions and to forgo some opportunities in favor of others for the long-term good of the institution. That is not a position that will necessarily make everyone happy, but it is one that is necessary.

As many leaders have found, though, this role is frequently more honored in theory than in practice, especially when pressures build from all sides. Across-the-board budget cuts are a prime example. Tempting as they are since they seem egalitarian, they are frequently disastrous for the institution in the long run since they tend to make weak areas weaker while sapping strength from stronger programs. Too many leaders fall into this trap; quite a few of them don't last long enough to make better choices.

I promised this book would take a practical, straightforward approach to the topic. But that doesn't mean that leading is easy. Neither are the tasks I've described above. Nevertheless, I believe that people new to leadership can acquire the skills necessary to do a more-than-adequate job. I also believe seasoned leaders can always learn more and become even better over time.

One way to begin the process is to take an inventory of personal strengths and weaknesses. Taking on the responsibility of leading requires that you know yourself well. No one person has all the necessary attributes for good leadership. Some of us lead better in one kind of situation than another. But all of us will do a better job if we become better acquainted with the person who lives inside our heads.

PERSONAL COMPETENCE

As I've noted, those who are searching for a step-by-step guidebook for good leadership will be disappointed in this book. My experience has shown me that becoming a better leader is an incremental process in which trial and error (especially error!) play important roles. But no one can hope to lead well without knowing which strategies and competencies fit his or her personal style and preferences. And that requires taking a personal inventory.

Is Wanting the Job Enough?

Simply wanting to be a leader is rarely sufficient for success. Over the years, I've seen only a slight relationship between career aspirations and good leading. Many deans, directors, department heads, and administrative vice presidents I've met have confided that they didn't start out wanting to occupy the top spot but "got stuck" with the job or sort of "happened into it." The number of leaders-by-default who were happy and those who were miserable were about equal. Even those who had worked hard to achieve a leadership position sort themselves pretty evenly between the comfortable and uncomfortable columns.

If a desire to lead isn't the most important factor, then what is? It turns out that leaders who knew themselves, their strengths, and their limitations were the most comfortable with their roles and the most successful at their jobs.

A Little Light Exercise

Getting to know who you are is always a good idea, no matter whether you work pretty much alone or with a variety of individuals or groups. But self-awareness is never more essential than for the person who must operate within the psychological fishbowl that accompanies any leadership position. If you are not aware of the less attractive parts of your personality (and everyone has them), you can be sure they will be pointed out to you, like it or not.

A good place to start is by creating a list of your strengths and weaknesses. Try to accomplish this task with as much objectivity as possible. Then ask several friends and colleagues, particularly those who have encouraged you to take on the tasks of leading, to check your work. Does your personal inventory jibe with theirs? Where are the discrepancies? Will the differences interfere with leading?

A colleague of mine completed this exercise with the pleasant discovery that she was goal-oriented, loyal, persuasive, collaborative, attentive to detail, and committed to fairness. However, she had to face the fact that she found dealing with personnel problems very difficult and frequently avoided confrontations when she feared feelings would be hurt.

Since most leaders will encounter delicate employee problems over the course of time, she knew she needed help in this area. This insight proved invaluable to what has become a very distinguished career to date.

Next, show your list to colleagues who know you but who are not close personal friends. Once again, examine the discrepancies among your list, your friends' lists, and your more distant colleagues' lists.

Sometimes would-be leaders are halted in their quest at this point. A former colleague who had been asked to consider a deanship was one of these. He encountered significant discrepancies in his inventory of skills and those others had written. I was one who counseled him to reject the offer, attractive though it was. Today he is a widely respected scholar and teacher with no regrets about the path he chose.

By now, you ought to have a far better idea of the difference between how you see yourself and how others see you. If there are wide discrepancies, you could assume that the world is crazy and you are the only sane person in it. That could be so, but think how frustrating it will be to lead all those crazy people out there.

If there is a strong correlation between your sense of self and that of others, then you can proceed confidently to step two. Now examine your strengths and weaknesses as they apply to the specific leadership responsibility at hand. How are you most effective when you work with people? Are you more task-oriented or more collegial in your approach? Will that style fit the group or groups to be led? Can you adapt your style to accommodate the work to be done?

Keep in mind that leading a group requires attending to both functional and social tasks. Social psychologists call them goal achievement and group maintenance. In the first task, the leader must find ways to motivate people to get the work done. The second task requires attending to the social and emotional needs of the group to achieve the cohesiveness and esprit de corps needed for ongoing effectiveness. Task-oriented leaders are often masters of efficiency and order, but they often face groups who resist and even sabotage their work because they feel devalued as people. Leaders who are very sensitive to human needs may have very happy people who never seem to get much work done.

Your style will lean in one direction or the other. No one has natural abilities in both areas. But I am convinced that your weaknesses in one area can be balanced with strengths in the other. Task-oriented leaders can raise their awareness of the expressive needs of the group. Intuitive leaders can acquire instrumental skills and increase the efficiency of their groups. And leaders of one stripe can hire or appoint assistants whose strengths complement their own. But the only way to achieve an effective balance is knowing yourself first.

Emotional Competence

Effective balance is more easily achieved when leaders continually work toward increasing their emotional competence. Fortunately, we are long past the time when we expected to leave all our feelings at the door when we came to work. Now, thanks to *Emotional Intelligence*[2] and *Working with Emotional Intelligence*[3] by Daniel Goleman, due attention is being given to our expressive nature, which follows us into the office, the laboratory, and the classroom like a lovable mutt who will not be left behind.

Emotional intelligence is linked to self-awareness. A person with high EQ (as opposed to IQ) knows what she or he is feeling and is able to take a step back to manage her or his reactions effectively. That doesn't mean giving vent to any feeling that comes along; it means acting or not acting on a feeling for the greater good of the group or in the best interests of an honest interpersonal relationship.

There are many brilliant people whose IQ scores are on the far right of the bell curve but who are emotionally "slow." They shine in the lab, are lauded by their peers, and produce truly cutting-edge work. But they are often very poor leaders.

Good leaders score high in the emotional intelligence category. They are self-aware, control impulses, can delay gratification, and are empathetic.

Studies show that these qualities correlate highly with the ability to motivate and work effectively with others—one writer labeled these people as the ones whose e-mail gets answered.

If you lead, your emotional competence is worth examining and improving as necessary. With a nod to the Menninger Foundation,[4] I offer the areas I believe are critical.

Ability to Deal Constructively with Reality

The opposite of this ability is called denial, a defense mechanism to shield us from the truth when to take it all in at once would be overwhelming. Think, for instance, of a patient who has just received the news of a serious disease. There may well be a period of disbelief and an unwillingness to act in his or her best interests—a smoker who has emphysema but continues to light up, or a runner whose knees are giving out but continues to log mile after mile.

Denial is often found in higher education, too. But while a period of emotional buffering may be called for, staying there is counterproductive. And leaders can afford only the shortest period of denial, if any. The same is true for marching to a different drummer—an admirable characteristic for the artist or writer, but a difficult one for a leader to maintain.

If you find yourself continually frustrated and angry because others cannot or will not accept your view of reality, then spend some time examining your ability to lead. You may be right, but that won't help you be a better leader. In fact, people see the most effective leaders as "one of us, but smarter, more skilled, and more visionary."

Capacity to Adapt to Change

Once upon a time, universities lived by the motto that "nothing new should happen for the first time here." All that tradition and school spirit was great, but it often stood in the way of necessary and beneficial adaptation. Today the pace of change is so accelerated that to resist it is akin to standing firm in the face of a hurricane, and just about as effective.

Leaders don't have the luxury of resisting change. They must anticipate the new, personally accommodate to the change, and then be ready to help others make the transition as smoothly as possible. Leaders who dawdle or give half-hearted support to change will be perceived as unconvinced and unconvincing. To a campus community that might really prefer to leave things alone, that's a deadly position.

Relative Freedom from Excessive Anxiety or Tension

This may seem unfair, especially when leading can actually cause these negative feelings. But the good leader understands that worry and stress use up a great deal of energy that would be far better spent on the work at hand. Constituents will be quick to pick up on the tension in the air and will also be rendered less effective. Leaders are duty bound to help others through the rough times, not make them worse. (I will deal with minimizing stress later.)

Capacity to Find Satisfaction in Both Giving and Receiving

No schoolchild escaped the injunction that it is better to give than to receive. And our Puritan forebears put selfishness right up there with the seven deadly sins. But I believe that the mature, emotionally competent person is as comfortable receiving a gift or compliment as she or he is bestowing the same on others. Children, for example, pass through a stage of helplessness, to wanting to "do it myself," and on to becoming able to help others. I think the final stage comes when we recognize we can't do everything ourselves and are comfortable seeking out support when we need it.

Ability to Form and Maintain Close Relationships with Others

Leaders must have a few trusted confidants to talk through the problems and concerns that are inevitable. The ability to open up and be honest with others is liberating and essential to good mental health. That doesn't mean burdening a large number of colleagues with your personal angst—in fact, that can be dangerous. But it does mean trusting a selected few and taking the risk of exposing doubts and fears. If you trust no one, can't accept another's vulnerabilities, or share your own, then you cannot be close to anyone. And, I venture to add, you will lack the essential humanness that all good leaders possess.

Ability to Differentiate between the Impossible and the Possible

In Alcoholics Anonymous this concept is grounded in the Serenity Prayer, which asks for acceptance of things one cannot change, courage to change the things one can, and wisdom to know the difference. Effective leaders have the capacity to select the doable tasks and move others in that direction. They also can identify those things that cannot be controlled and convey that truth in a way that brings relief rather than continued frustration.

Ability to Redirect Hostile Energy into Constructive Outlets

It is not events that give us problems but rather our reactions to them. Anger, for example, is normal and even healthy when it motivates us to make a necessary change. But living in a constant state of anger is draining not only for ourselves but also for those around us. Finding ways to redirect, rather than suppress, negative feelings into a constructive or creative activity such as exercise, writing, or music is essential for effective leadership.

Capacity to Love Oneself and to Love Others

In my capacity as a leader in various guises, I've found myself subjected to what I call the fame/shame syndrome. (See some fine examples of this syndrome in appendix B.) I've been praised for accomplishments that weren't mine and damned for mistakes that I didn't make. As I moved up the higher education ladder, I found that my jokes were much funnier in social situations and the venom in editorials castigating me much more bitter. Had I not had a good sense of who I was and a capacity to love that self, warts and all, I could have been badly misled by external events. In fact, lack of self-love almost always leads to a destructive dependency on the opinions of others for self-worth.

Lack of self-love is also strongly linked to an inability to love others. And if we cannot give or receive love, we are incapacitated as leaders. Loving means giving, acknowledging feelings, seeing that there is more to the world than that which can be verified by the senses, and allowing this most powerful emotion to pervade our working lives as well as our personal lives.

Willingness to Self-Evaluate

Those who grow as leaders develop a capacity to hear criticism and evaluate its truth and worth. Not everything that's offered to us is valid, but knowing what is requires an ability to be introspective and self-correcting.

I hasten to add that there are no leaders who have all these qualities nailed down. Some are very good at one skill but struggle with another. Some leaders are lovable hotheads who seem to need to blow their stacks once in a while but are also excellent evaluators of that which cannot be changed and that which can. Others have a hard time managing their anxiety occasionally but are quick to empathize with others and meet their needs.

Nevertheless, leaders need to remain aware of their relative emotional competencies and work to improve those areas that remain problematic.

to follow someone who has a good understanding of where the institution should go and a road map to get there.

Making a difference requires that you set an example. It won't be enough to call for smaller classes for all your students, for instance. You will have to provide the resources that make this happen and support the people who will do the work. You might even decide to teach one or two of these classes yourself.

Making a difference does not often provide instant gratification, however. Leading in a complex environment like higher education is a long, slow process, and gains may not be visible for years or decades to come. If you can't accept the results in the form of a legacy, you may want to think again about taking on this risky and sometimes frustrating calling.

If you don't share these core beliefs, leadership in higher education may not be worth it for you. For me the rewards are great. If you think so too, read on.

NOTES

1. "Leadership and Power," *Leadership Papers*, Number 1, Washington, D.C.: Independent Sector, 1986.
2. Daniel Goleman, *Emotional Intelligence*, New York: Bantam Books, 1995.
3. Daniel Goleman, *Working with Emotional Intelligence*, New York: Bantam Books, 1998.
4. William C. Menninger, "Criteria of Emotional Maturity," Topeka, Kans.: Menninger Foundation, 1966.

CHAPTER 3

Interpersonal Competence

Such is the human race. Often it seems a pity that Noah ... didn't miss the boat.

—Mark Twain

Once grounded in a solid sense of self and possessed of a willingness to upgrade continually their personal competencies, leaders know they have to take that show on the road. And that means getting out there and dealing with human beings, with all the stubbornness, hidden agendas, hypersensitivities, quirks, and axes to grind that it entails.

But work with people we must. Very few leaders can be truly successful without the support, collaboration, and goodwill of many hundreds of others. That has been true in my case and in all of the other leaders' situations I have had a chance to observe and read about. Splendid isolation has its virtues; good leadership, though, is not one of them.

Then, too, a good idea often becomes a great one when treated with the insights, observations, and enhancements that only a gathering of similarly committed colleagues can provide. I think most of us want and need the approval and even the criticism of our peers and would much rather consult with others than go out there and tilt at windmills all by ourselves.

KNOWING THE PLAYERS

The groups of players on the higher education field are diverse in both composition and agendas. Leaders are well advised to become familiar with each group's expectations, as well as their own. That is not to say that you will fulfill them; it means that you will be balancing these needs and desires and meeting them when and if they fit within your institution's mission and vision.

Faculty

Central to any learning community, faculty members provide the intellectual resources to create knowledge, help students learn, and apply knowledge to practical purposes for the greater good. Even if success eludes you in other areas, if you hire and retain a good faculty, things will work out for you.

Faculty expect to be kept informed and involved in decisions that affect them. They also expect reasonable compensation and the infrastructure necessary to do their work. They expect you to serve as an advocate for higher education and for their particular interests. And they expect you to be available always.

You can expect the faculty to excel not only in their disciplines but also as citizens of the institutional community. They should demonstrate willingness to serve your institution by supporting its mission and serving their students.

Faculty are disappointed when you fail to be their head cheerleader, particularly when they perceive that their compensation is seriously inadequate. They are disappointed when their time is consumed with trivial committee work (even when they suggested it), when decisions are made in isolation, when the institution seems adrift, and when you aren't always available.

You may be disappointed when the faculty refuse to take responsibility for the institution's welfare, when they refuse to consider any meaningful changes, when their loyalty is primarily to their disciplines, and when they complain that you are not available.

Students

If the faculty is central to your mission, then students are the catalysts that make things happen. They are both colleagues in the search for knowledge and customers whose tuition dollars keep the institution running. We take them as they are and try our best to earn their faith and their parents' faith in what we provide.

They expect a good education at a reasonable cost. They expect fair treatment, respect, and understanding as they meet the challenge of financing their studies, managing their time, and emerging into adulthood all at once. They also expect you to be available.

You can expect them to be good citizens, to be as interested in learning as they are in their future economic success, and to be honest and diligent.

Students are disappointed when they believe they are paying too much for their education, when the faculty and staff invest too little in their needs, and when there is little congruence between rhetoric and reality. And they are disappointed when you are not available.

You may be disappointed when they seem unwilling to think beyond the present cost of their education, when they sacrifice true learning in favor of expediency, and when they are less than honest in their quest for personal advancement.

Board Members

One of the reasons higher education in the United States is the best in the world is the presence of volunteer boards made up of men and women who agree to guide their institutions on matters of policy and direction. Of course, this system isn't perfect and problems do arise. Still, it works more often than not.

Board members expect to be made aware of challenges that face their institution and to have leaders who articulate the institution's mission and vision and make hard decisions. They expect to be involved fully in policy issues. They also expect you to be available to them.

You can expect your board to provide you with guidance and support, to stick to those concerns that are within their jurisdiction, and to be available when you need them.

Board members may be disappointed when you can't seem to get the job done, when you avoid hard decisions, when you've collected too many enemies (even when that may be justified), and when the institution seems to be adrift. They really don't like surprises, and they are upset when you aren't available to them.

You may be disappointed when board members try to micromanage, when they interfere with academic freedom, and when they don't support you in times of crisis.

Alumni

The men and women who call your institution "alma mater" can and should be your most enthusiastic cheerleaders. They can also be the best public relations representatives both in their own personal success and in the good words they spread about your institution.

Alumni expect to be kept informed, to have your loyalty, and to have more resources to support their agendas. They also expect you to be available.

You can expect them to remain loyal and supportive and, eventually, to provide significant financial support. You can also hope for their success since their good fortune speaks well for the education they earned at your institution.

They may be disappointed when they find it difficult to take pride in their school, when they can't find ways to become involved, and when the institution seems to be adrift. They will be disappointed if you limit your contacts with them.

You may be disappointed when alumni seem to be more concerned with Saturday's football score than the institution's mission and vision and when they seem unwilling to offer financial support necessary to insure the future.

Government

While public institutions depend on public funds for the lion's share of their resources, private institutions also look to state and federal government for support. Smooth government relations, then, are essential for nearly all of higher education.

Government officials expect your institution to stick to its mission, to deliver high-quality education as cheaply as possible, and to add to the state and national prestige with significant research and service (provided these don't cost too much). They also want you to be available.

You can expect them to like you but to be cynical about your motives, often seeing higher education as no different from all the other social institutions making demands on the public treasury. Nevertheless, you can expect them to provide you with support, to understand your particular mission, and to reflect the importance of your mission with sufficient resources.

Government officials are disappointed when their constituents complain loudly about the price of tuition (or about anything else that disrupts their political lives), when it appears that insufficient resources are being directed toward teaching, and when your institution seems to demand preferential treatment, especially when compared with such legitimate needs as child care and medical care. And they will protest that you are not available to them.

You may be disappointed when they don't provide you with the resources necessary to carry out your mission and, instead, impose burdensome bureaucratic controls. You may also be disappointed when politicians use your institution as a means to advance their own agendas.

There are other constituencies, of course, and each will demand that you exercise world-class interpersonal skills. And, while you will deal with each group slightly differently, the guidelines below will work time after time. Not that you will please everyone all the time. There will be times when one group's gain is, indeed, another group's loss.

INDISPENSABLE SKILLS

You can succeed if you create environments in which collaboration and cooperation can thrive. Just as personal competencies can be improved and supplemented, so too can the ability to work effectively with individuals and groups. The following sections describe some of the skills that I and others have found to be indispensable.

Ability to Deal Creatively and Effectively with Conflict

Expecting to lead without encountering conflict is right up there with believing in the Easter bunny. Differences are a natural part of human interaction. That is as true when two friends are trying to decide which movie to see as when an entire university is coming to grips with restructuring in the face of economic challenges.

I'll go further and say that conflict can often stimulate us to work smarter than we would otherwise. The energy that comes from differences between and among people can be a very positive force.

That's not to say that leaders are advised to stir up conflict when it doesn't exist. Rather, they need to know how to manage conflict when it arises. That doesn't mean you should stifle conflict or avoid conflict. It means you should move people toward consensus. Not everyone will be completely happy with the outcome, but it should be possible for everyone to buy into the options selected for the good of the organization.

Very few would-be leaders have solid conflict management skills. Those who do and who are willing to learn more are in great demand. I'll offer more specific advice later.

Ability to Deal Effectively with Groups

Leaders with experience are quick to point out that more than one-third of their time is spent in groups of people. That's not news. But in spite of that easily verifiable fact, group work elicits more groans than cheers in anticipation. Committees tend to bumble along, taking hours and days to accomplish the smallest of tasks. Meetings drag on, sans agenda or even a semblance of efficiency, engendering frustration, boredom, and sometimes stonewalling. Yet we form new committees and call more meetings as if just doing so will make things better. It won't, and the leader who knows how to run an effective group has great advantages over those who remain clueless. I treat working with groups in more detail later.

Ability to Listen

Once again, this is a skill that is universally praised but hardly ever practiced. No wonder. It takes a strong person to tune in to what others are really saying, to let another finish without butting in, and to exercise the patience that allows true communication to happen. All too often, our tendency is to use the time during which another is speaking to formulate our argument for when it comes our time to speak.

Good listening skills are essential to good decisions. In fact, I don't think consensus is possible without them.

Ability to Be Assertive with People at All Levels

Good leaders treat their peers and those whose positions are above and below them on the flow chart pretty much the same. They are assertive rather than aggressive, they make their objectives clear, and they avoid manipulation or intimidation. They can work with those who have the power to hire and fire without obsequiousness and without fear. At the same time, they avoid coming across as patronizing to those with less power and authority.

Ability to Move Others to "Yes"

Working with others is almost never a neat, tidy, linear process. Rather than lockstepping through agendas, human beings have a tendency to get stuck for a variety of reasons. These include those tricky hidden agendas, insufficient information, the presence of opposing factions, or downright boredom. Leaders need to be able to work through an impasse efficiently but without bruising egos or ignoring certain points of view.

Ability to Use Power Effectively

Power has earned a bad rep. Think of terms like *power mad, control freak,* and *Machiavellian*. Nevertheless, power always lodges somewhere. Why not acknowledge it, claim it, and use it for good? Leaders who empower themselves are able to guide others toward shared goals. As with all the other skills, this one can be learned and improved.

Ability to Motivate Others

It may be stressing the obvious, but leaders are there to—well, lead. Your job is not to carry on fascinating conversations, show off your inherent brilliance, or sharpen the pencils. You have to get out there and motivate the people who chose you. That means encouraging, praising, redirecting, humoring, reflecting, and sometimes criticizing them. It means staying on top of the task and supplying the energy that may lag at times. Above all, it means staying positive, certain in the conviction that all the hard work will prove its worth.

While I consider all of the seven interpersonal skills listed above essential and teachable, four can make or break good leadership. They are dealing with conflict, the power to lead, motivating others, and working with groups. I deal with the first three in this chapter, but the last is so important that I devote all of chapter 4 to it.

DEALING WITH CONFLICT

If I had one piece of advice for any new leader, it would be, "Expect conflict." Certainly in times of crisis and often in times of calm, differences of opinion, competing claims on resources, personality clashes, and other points of friction will surface. Leaders who try to suppress this inevitable fact of human interaction are doomed to frustration that comes from wasted efforts.

Conflict well managed, however, can enrich an organization. From the heat and energy generated by the sharpened thinking and brisk discussions that conflict engenders can come the new ideas that move everyone forward. Naturally, leaders must take care that conflict does not become a personal attack or a vehicle for a clique's agenda.

Leaders must remain a stabilizing force throughout the conflict process. This is true when the leader stands outside the arena as a disinterested party, but especially when he or she is an integral part of the conflict.

Sensitive to the point at which the "buck has stopped," the leader must be ready to step in and make a firm decision when necessary.

One model that has helped me understand the process categorizes conflict as collegial, complete, or strategic. Each type of conflict is legitimate and part of any organization's life. Leaders should learn how to deal with each.

The Collegial Model

This kind of conflict is the most benign. It calls up a picture of intelligent, well-meaning individuals who put forth reasoned points of view and then come together in complete accord. And that does happen sometimes!

This model works when all participants share a common set of values and goals. Opposing sides can be quite passionate in their beliefs, but the individual members are conscious that it is the good of the organization that must be served.

Leaders play a facilitator role in this kind of conflict. They keep participants moving forward by reminding them of the common goals, by making certain that all parties get a fair hearing, and by indicating the points where all agree and where disagreements remain.

The emerging consensus will seem a natural outgrowth of the process, a happy result that the leader can enjoy for as long as he or she can. Would that all conflicts could be resolved in this way! Of course, they can't, and leaders must not feel like failures when the heat rises in the room as arguments become protracted. Sometimes consensus isn't possible.

The Complete Conflict (Zero-Sum) Model

Sometimes one side will win and the other will lose. Some choices have consequences that cannot be modified or adapted to meet everyone's needs. For example, suppose a university is contemplating the closure of a program that is expensive to maintain and that yields little in revenue. Given the highly specialized nature of academic work, closing will mean the end of certain faculty and staff careers on that campus. Still, closure may well be the best resolution for the institution as a whole. Good leaders know they must be willing to choose the best option, leave no room for compromise when none can be made, and keep the organization on track.

It is important in a zero-sum game like this that leaders constantly check their own motives for ego involvement or vindictiveness. If members of the organization detect this personal association, they will quickly delegitimize the decision. Instead, leaders should remain detached but open, and make certain that the decision is understood if not entirely accepted.

The Strategic Model

The labor-management negotiation process is a good example of this kind of conflict. Like the collegial model, the strategic model begins with all parties participating in discussion. But instead of consensus, each side needs to give a little to reach resolution. In the end, none will be entirely satisfied, but all should be able to buy into and support the decision.

Leaders in this process keep all participants involved, avoid arguments that escalate into personal attacks, and remain detached, as in the previous models. Here they also help participants isolate the points of agreement and then focus on the areas of genuine conflict. Then leaders serve as the mediators who help compromises emerge and become accepted.

New leaders struggle most often to stick to the collegial or strategic models in conflict situations since these seem to be the most civilized and least messy. But this isn't always possible or even desirable. Even in the hallowed reaches of the academic department or the university boardroom, measured progress through a bloodless collegial meeting is not the norm. Give-and-take happens. If it didn't, the sometimes glacial pace of change in academe would surely come to a complete stop.

Even give-and-take doesn't work sometimes. In an effort to expand opportunities for women athletes, one institution elected to divert athletic dollars to this end for capital and operating expenses. It also determined that no institutional dollars would be provided to fill the shortfall that would occur in the men's athletic programs. The president decided that a 20 percent across-the-board cut was in order.

Then the non-revenue sports like rowing and volleyball lost their competitive edge, and the money-generating sports like football and men's basketball slipped precipitously in their respective national rankings. In fact, the entire university athletic program became an embarrassment to students, alumni, and community members. All because the president and her administrators refused to make the courageous, zero-sum choice—cut two men's programs, withstand the firestorm of criticism that would follow, and move forward.

The Four-Step Process

I advise leaders to guide their constituents through a four-step process that works consistently, if not perfectly, to help manage conflict.

1. Listen to the other side
2. Repeat what you have heard
3. Indicate areas of agreement
4. Finally, isolate the true areas of disagreement

The first three steps frequently work magic in an emotionally intense situation. By insisting on listening, repeating, and agreeing, the leader can very effectively sweep away issues that aren't relevant to the problem at hand. It's amazing how fast grudges, personality issues, and other unproductive matters wither under the light of systematic approaches like this one. Often the areas of agreement surprise participants and help them come together in far more productive ways.

With the areas of disagreement sharply defined, work can begin to reach consensus. When there are more than two people involved, leaders must practice their group skills to manage the conflict. (See chapter 4 for details.)

With two combatants, the process is simplified. I've seen it played out beautifully, especially if the leader can interject a touch of dramatic flair. Two administrators at a leading institution could almost never agree. What one saw as light, the other saw as dark. Their personalities were at polar opposites and neither missed an opportunity to malign the other. Both were anxious to see the president about a pressing issue, but of course wanted a private audience. The issue, however, involved both their areas, so the president insisted that it be a three-person meeting.

The first administrator took the floor with a lengthy explanation of the problem. The other butted in from time to time or indicated his disgust with facial expressions and body language. The president halted the monologue by asking the other party if she understood what was being said. With a nod to the first person's argument, she launched into her own interpretation full speed ahead.

At this point, the president rose up in righteous indignation and with a tone that allowed for no argument, she said, "I have never encountered such unprofessional behavior in my entire career. You two can't seem to occupy the same space, let alone work together for the institution. I will not stand for any more of this bickering. I am tired of problems hanging on for weeks and months just because you two prefer to undercut each other!"

Stating that there was agreement on the nature of the problem, she then demanded that the two administrators meet later to discuss possible solutions they could agree on and to list solutions they could not agree on. For the latter, she asked them to come to consensus on the pros and cons of each of the disputed solutions. This was to be in writing and produced within 48 hours. At a meeting upon the submission of the report, the president promised the conflict would be resolved in less than 10 minutes.

The meeting never happened. The two administrators resolved all their differences and designed a common approach to the problem. They still didn't like each other, but they learned that this leader wasn't ever going to let conflicts simmer for long without intervening.

THE POWER TO LEAD

Some of my most stimulating conversations have centered around the topic of power. To many in higher education, using power is manipulative and beneath the dignity of a leader. Some well-meaning people believe that decisions must always come from the meeting of great minds, no matter how long it takes to achieve consensus or no matter how trivial the choice to be made. Others believe that ignoring power is playing the leadership game without all the pieces, like playing chess minus the queen. It is possible to win, but much more difficult.

I give due credit to my good friend Jim Fisher, former president of Towson State University and of the Center for the Advancement and Support of Education (CASE), for shaping my views of power in a college or university. He and I have devoted many hours to discussing the subject. I have given many more to reading and re-reading his writings in this area. Naturally I also rely on my own experiences with, and observations of, the exercise of power as it relates to leadership.

Fisher defines power as A's ability to move B to act, whether or not B wants to do so. David McClelland suggests that power is a more important attribute of leadership than the need for personal success, the desire to work and be with people, or the need for approval.[1] I've heard it said that the powerful can be boring at a cocktail party and other people think it's their fault.

Power does exist. Weak leaders refuse to admit this or are unwilling to exert power. They often lose influence, sometimes to others less able to keep the whole of the institution in perspective. Strong leaders are comfortable with power and use this tool wisely, effectively, and humanely.

Sources of Power

There are several sources of power, some useful and others not, at least not in the long term. Fisher borrows from the paradigm created by sociologists J.R.P. French and B. Raven to explain these sources and their consequences.[2]

Coercive Power

This is the least effective but, sadly, the most used kind of power. It relies on threats and punishment to bring compliance. Leaders most comfortable with this kind of power blame, control, and second-guess their staffs. Unfortunately it works, at least for a while. But in the long term, coercive power fails to lead to real success. People have a variety of ways to subvert this kind of leadership through shoddy work, forgetfulness, health problems, and sometimes outright sabotage. Sanctions are sometimes necessary when individuals routinely fail to meet their responsibilities. They should always be the last resort, rather than a continuing source of fear and grudging acceptance.

Reward Power

At the opposite end of the spectrum is the power that derives from recognition, promotion, praise, and favors. As good parents know, rewarding good behavior is usually more effective than punishing bad behavior. But even this kind of power has limits. Fisher found no evidence that reward power alone could ensure long-lasting loyalty or commitment to an institutional cause. Part of the problem is that no reward can ever be enough, especially in a knowledge industry like higher education. In these environments, more than 75 percent of the people believe they are in the top 10 percent of intelligence and performance. Rewards lose their power when the Lake Wobegon effect is present—"where all the women are strong, all the men are good looking, and all the children are above average."

Legitimate Power

The source of this power is the position itself. Chancellors, provosts, deans, vice presidents, department heads, office managers, and others derive some of their legitimacy from the job they hold and the tradition that accompanies it. Wise leaders use this form of power as a platform for the structure and authority they need. It is true that power derived from a position has eroded in higher education over the years, as has been true in virtually every area of human endeavor. Each new administration in Washington, for example, seems to have a bit less clout than the one previous to it as the electorate grows increasingly cynical about its leaders. Still, legitimate power does exist and can prove useful, if not entirely sufficient, for good leadership.

Legitimate power, then, can command respect and influence. It is not to be taken lightly and certainly not given away. It is regrettable that many leaders comport themselves in such a way as to diminish their authority either by becoming overly familiar in their interactions or refusing to stand on ceremony when ceremony would actually be a very good place to stand. Once given away, legitimate power never comes back.

Expert Power

Defined as influence derived from knowing what you're doing, expert power is rarely questioned if the expertise is real. (I never question the computer gurus on my campus, for instance. But I have a suspicion that they keep one step ahead of us just so they can smile benignly when we mess up.) Expert power makes it possible for consultants to work in organizations in which they have no lasting association. Expert power is accorded the group treasurer whose knowledge of the assets and liabilities is taken as gospel. Expert power is available to the person with natural energy and superior social skills who can serve as a group facilitator or trainer. Alas, most of us have expertise in only one or two areas, if we're lucky. Thus, good leaders strive to appear knowledgeable in their areas but feel secure enough to delegate the details to others. They also know enough to stay out of areas where only their ignorance will be on display.

Charismatic Power

By force of their presence, energy, and vision, charismatic leaders inspire others to follow. At the very least they have respect; at most, they are revered. Some believe charisma is an innate quality. Others maintain that it can be developed and nurtured. Fisher goes further by naming charismatic power as the most important kind. Certainly this force is difficult to sustain in the long run. If familiarity doesn't exactly breed contempt, it often tarnishes the halo that many leaders sport at the beginning of their tenure. Charisma slippage is also one of the reasons many leaders in higher education have shorter terms of office these days. Once off the pedestal, it's very difficult to climb back up.

Fisher states that maintaining charisma requires a certain social distance from followers. That is, exercising this kind of power means staying close enough to the group and the institution to establish personal identification, but sufficiently removed to be inspiring. Social distance need not be cold and forbidding. In fact, leaders can and should be warm, friendly, genuine, and concerned. Still they need to avoid the over-familiarity than can diminish power. Says Fisher, "Nice guys, at least to the degree they compromise their office, do finish last."

There are some leaders today who manage long-term, effective administrations in higher education. These are the ones who make use of their charisma at the beginning to gain the confidence of their constituencies and then rely more heavily on their legitimate and expert powers. Some might say that the aura of invincibility wears off over time; I maintain that charisma can last if it is solidly grounded in honesty, expertise, and legitimacy.

Power, then, is inherent in the task of leading. It pays to understand it and use it wisely. For more information about power in higher education, I recommend *The Power of the Presidency and Presidential Leadership: Making a Difference* by James L. Fisher.[3]

Exercising Power

Sometimes it's easier to see things in the negative rather than the positive. For example, a former colleague simply couldn't fit the concept of power into his ethical system. To him, any exercise of power was distastefully manipulative. But he found himself continually outpaced by situations that grew quickly out of control. Others moved in to take over, leaving him with a lesson to be learned in leadership. I'm glad to say that he didn't make the same mistakes at his next post.

Another colleague practiced coercive power with a vengeance. He was undone when his accrediting body came for a visit and found that virtually everyone on campus had little to talk about except the sick environment his tactics had created. The university had become a place where people struggled to respond to each new edict from on high. The fear of punishment had crushed all sense of collegiality, loyalty, or commitment.

Another leader would have preferred walking barefoot on broken glass to using coercion of any kind. Yet when faced with a colleague who had been publicly defiant and disloyal, she acted immediately by firing him and demanding that his desk be cleared out by the end of that very workday. She never had to resort to this tactic again since the community learned from this example that she could act decisively on personnel matters when necessary.

I've observed reward power gone amok in the guise of a college president whose obsession was improving his institution's evaluation system so that high achievers could be publicly and lavishly praised. This worked for those who are motivated that way. But for those who found rewards in other ways, the method was ineffectual.

Another president was universally admired for his expert power. He worked harder than anyone else and absorbed new information quickly. He also had a long history with his institution and a deep commitment to its welfare. Yet he was charismatically challenged and wouldn't have fit anyone's concept of a powerful figure. Nevertheless, in action he had an aura about him that convinced and comforted others. He was very success-ful; well-wishers lined up to brush the lint from his suits.

MOTIVATING OTHERS

Making leadership meaningful requires the support of those who are led. Without a strong following, leaders might as well pack it in. And that requires knowing how to motivate others to join you in carrying out your organization's particular mission and vision. That doesn't mean charging full steam ahead. If you do, you'll find you're out there all alone.

The first step is discovering what your followers need and want. One way to do that is to understand the exchange theory of human relationships. Simply put, we are motivated to action when we believe there will be a reward of some sort—not necessarily monetary, depending on the situa-tion. Crudely put, the exchange theory is a sophisticated answer to the question, "What's in it for me?"

While most of us don't keep score, we know at some level that human interaction involves hundreds of exchanges. Even if we don't have a tally sheet of puts and takes, we do understand who is giving and who is receiving in each interaction. Not all relationships average the magic 50-50, but if the exchange rate stays at 90-10 or 80-20 with the leader at the receiving end, those who follow will have little motivation to do one more thing for "the Gipper."

I think we don't give our children all the information when we tell them that it is better to give than to receive. We ought to add that giving is not only a right and moral thing to do and a satisfying act in and of itself, it is also returned in kind eventually. With all those givers out there, there have to be receivers. The saying "what goes around, comes around" is not only apt as a warning to those who cheat, lie, and steal; it is also an incentive to givers.

If you would understand exchange theory, spend some time observing a state or federal legislative session in action. Politicians know without ever stating it that supporting a colleague's bill today has a very good chance of being reciprocated somewhere down the line.

College campuses, on the other hand, have been described as organized anarchies. The internal politics can change depending on who wants what at a particular time. Faculty members who have little to do with each other most of the time may form a coalition against a threat to academic freedom. Students who devote most of their time to studying and socializing may become quite vocal about a perceived dereliction of duty by the administration and band together in protest.

Leaders, then, must understand and work with exchanges in human interaction. A paradigm drawn by management scholars Cohen and Bradford is helpful.

Currencies

As you can see, in this model, motivators are labeled "currencies" (see page 37). Knowing which currencies are most valuable to an individual or group is an important part of good leadership. And currencies can gain or lose value depending on the situation and the fact that individuals can be motivated by more than one kind.

The several *inspiration-related currencies* can be used nearly universally, even though a small number of people will never be moved by a higher order of rewards. These currencies include the institution's mission and vision, the call to excellence, and the moral imperative. As a leader, your job is to inspire through articulation and example.

Task-related currencies appeal to people who find satisfaction in a job well done. They feel good about themselves when the report is finished, the students are registered, or the sidewalks are plowed. They are motivated by resources to improve their performance. Greater prestige, a salary increase, opportunities for further education, greater access to information, and a larger staff to help are all strong incentives in this category.

Position-related currencies single out good work in a public way. Motivators in this group include promotions, title upgrades, awards, citations, and publicity. Recognition protocols, press releases, and other forms of acknowledgment let people know their contributions are valuable. In turn, they are motivated to further improve their efforts in the hope of more to come.

CURRENCIES FREQUENTLY VALUED IN ORGANIZATIONS

Inspiration-Related Currencies

Vision	Being involved in a task that has larger significance for unit, organization, constituents, or society
Excellence	Having a chance to do important things really well
Moral/Ethical Correctness	Doing what is right by a higher standard than efficiency

Task-Related Currencies

New Resources	Obtaining money, budget increases, personnel, space, etc.
Challenge/Learning Assistance	Getting help with existing projects or unwanted tasks
Task Support	Receiving overt or subtle backing or actual assistance with implementation
Rapid Response	Quicker response time
Information	Access to organizational as well as technical knowledge

Position-Related Currencies

Recognition	Acknowledgment of effort, accomplishment, or abilities
Visibility	The chance to be known by higher-ups or significant others in the organization
Reputation	Being seen as competent, committed
Insider/Importance	A sense of belonging to inner circle
Contacts	Links to others

Relationship-Related Currencies

Understanding	Having concerns and issues listened to
Acceptance/Inclusion	Closeness and friendship
Personal support	Personal and emotional backing

Personal-Related Currencies

Gratitude	Appreciation or expression of indebtedness
Ownership/Involvement	Ownership of and influence over important tasks
Self-Concept	Affirmation of one's values, self-esteem, and identity
Comfort	Avoidance of roadblocks and other hassles

Source: Allan Cohen and David Bradford, *Influence without Authority*, 1990. Reprinted by permission of John Wiley and Sons, New York.

Relationship-related currencies are rewards for those who value a sympathetic ear, personal support, a note of thanks, and other kinds of interpersonal connections. These are more important when they come from the leader. As I have stated earlier, though, leaders need to walk a fine line between genuine friendliness and over-familiarity. The latter nearly always leads to a serious diminution of influence. Nevertheless, I believe it is possible to provide personal attention and appreciation to those who need it.

Leaders must take note of and respond to the various currencies or exchanges that help people want to come to work and do their best. Once again, excesses are possible. Leading by inspiration alone can backfire if it stops at rhetoric. One university leader I know was widely acclaimed for his inspirational speeches. In fact, his words were often cited in the *Chronicle of Higher Education* and in the popular press. However, since nothing much ever got done on his campus; he was more influential externally than at home.

Another colleague was a master at relationship currencies. He tried never to miss a birthday celebration, memorial service, pre-game rally, and the like. He encouraged others to follow suit so that eventually it was a rare week that didn't have a social event of some sort on campus. He found himself feeling constantly overburdened by his social calendar and frustrated that he never seemed to have the time for working on harder issues. In time, he was discounted as a nice but ineffectual guy.

Here's how good use of currencies can look. At the annual speech to the faculty, the president outlines the challenges for the coming year, placing them in the context of current events in higher education and the broader vision for her institution's future. While the talk has inspirational elements, it also invites the audience to understand the leader's sense of the institution and to join in moving it forward. As follow-up, this leader then challenges her team of administrators to set forth initiatives designed to implement this forward movement. Some of these initiatives she supports with extra funding. Early achievements in this direction are publicly rewarded and praised, in the hope of inspiring still more to come. Individuals are recognized with personal thanks from the president where and when appropriate. It is a successful year, engineered to a large degree by the judicious use of currencies.

Motivational Guidelines

Along with currencies, leaders can also follow some proven motivational guidelines as suggested by Cohen and Bradford.[4]

- Mutual respect. Assume the people you work with are competent and intelligent. Even if you suspect they aren't, you're better off starting from this perspective. If this turns out to be a false assumption later on, you can change your strategy. Begin by finding out things about group members that you can admire. The person who moves slowly and methodically, for example, may keep the group on track. The person who seems sloppy and scattered at times may have very creative ideas to offer. This is difficult to do when the leader's style clashes with the group's expectations, but it's well worth attempting, since offering respect is usually returned in kind.

- Openness. Assume that straight talk is in everyone's best interest. Withholding necessary information nearly always backfires. People become suspicious and assume the worst. Sometimes information can be hard to swallow. One university recently broke with a long-standing tradition and essentially opened its books to the community during a time of financial challenge. Some groups became defensive because their areas were shown to be underproductive. Others tended toward smugness because their departments were showing "profits." Eventually, the campus settled down to the work at hand—helping the university meet the challenge and move forward. This formidable job was made easier with shared information.

- Trust. Start with the assumption that no one you work with is there to hurt you. You may be betrayed later on. If so, you can deal with the situation when it arises. But starting out by second-guessing everyone's intentions will stimulate paranoia and fear, not an atmosphere conducive to good work. As a leader, you also have to be trustworthy, a state you will reach if you follow through, remain honest, put in the time, and offer your energy and enthusiasm.

- Mutual benefit. Assume that the people you lead want to succeed as much as you do. Base your working relationships on the idea that you are all in this together. Through your understanding of the currencies group members value, you can help each person find the kind of satisfaction he or she needs, in addition to the positive feelings nearly everyone has when furthering a cause they believe in.

Now that your personal competencies are in order, it's time to move from the locker room into the arena where groups of people do the work of the institution. In chapter 4 you will find a guide to the competencies that will enable you to work effectively with small and large groups, skills that may well give you a distinct advantage over those who would leap from personal skills into the task of leading the whole institution all at once.

NOTES

1. "The Two Faces of Power," *Journal of International Affairs* 24 (1969): 141–54.
2. "The Bases of Social Power," in *Studies in Social Power*, edited by D. Cartwright, Ann Arbor, Mich.: University of Michigan Press and Institute for Social Research, 1959.
3. James L. Fisher, *The Power of the Presidency and Presidential Leadership: Making a Difference*, New York: Macmillan and American Council on Education, 1984.
4. Allan Cohen and David Bradford, *Influence without Authority*, New York: John Wiley and Sons, 1990.

CHAPTER 4

Group Knowledge

A committee is a cul de sac to which ideas are lured and then quietly strangled.

—John A. Lincoln

All the interpersonal skill in the world won't help you unless you know something about group dynamics, structures, functions, and roles. Remember, you'll spend more than a third of your time in a group as leader and participant. Unfortunately, groups have become easy targets for blame and ridicule. You have, no doubt, heard the saying, "A committee is a group of the unfit, appointed by the unwilling, to do the unnecessary." Or the definition of a committee as "a group of individuals who can do nothing and then meet collectively to decide that nothing can be done." If not these, then you must have heard that "a camel is a horse designed by a committee."

Why all these derisive comments? In part, they exist because of mismanagement, unclear objectives, and poor leadership. Under these conditions, groups can be ineffective, stultifying, time-wasting, and even destructive.

Leaders who take the time to learn more about groups, though, can help them become efficient, effective, creative, innovative, and legitimizing for major decisions. Not only do I believe that is possible, I've seen it happen time after time.

There are three critical elements to understanding groups: their purpose, their functions, and their size. These may seem absurdly simple, but I am amazed at the number of committees, task forces, and study groups that are assembled without attention to one, two, or all three of these elements.

The result is confusion at best, and at worst, a great deal of lost time and money.

GROUP PURPOSE

As a leader, you must be able to articulate the purpose of your group, team, or committee. It's best, if you can do so in as few words as possible since short statements are easier to keep in mind, the better to serve as a measure for the group's progress.

A clear purpose is also essential to keep members involved and committed. Research bears this out. We are told that people need four factors to motivate them to remain engaged: purpose, an incentive to belong to the group, tasks that are challenging but not overwhelming, and a sense that their work is directly related to the purpose. Some basic group purposes follow.

Giving Information

The group assembles at a particular place and time to hear the leader make some sort of formal (and sufficiently important) announcement or explanation. Usually there is an opportunity for members to ask questions and for the leader to respond. This is particularly desirable if the information is sensitive and could stimulate panic and rumors.

Like the boy who cried wolf, leaders need to avoid summoning the troops for this purpose too frequently. Such meetings can lose their impact if called too often, causing participants either to avoid them or to use the time to doodle and daydream, all the while feeling frustrated that their time is being wasted.

Sharing Information

This two-way process keeps all members informed. Participants' contributions are as important, if not more important, than the leader's words of wisdom. This purpose fits under the category of "keeping the lines of communication open." Note that this is not a time for major decisions to be made, although some conclusions may arise naturally. As with the one-way information-sharing process, this purpose can be accomplished in a short period of time.

Fortunately today technology can serve as the conduit for a great deal of information-sharing via e-mail and fax. Internet list-serves and distribution lists can take the place of many meetings, reserving face-to-face time for more active work.

Decision Making

This may seem to be the obvious purpose of any group. Unfortunately there are too many meetings called in which information is given, received, shared, discussed, written about, and so on, but no concrete decisions made nor any clear direction set. This is where good leadership makes a difference. Skilled leaders know how to set an agenda, facilitate discussion, and help the group arrive at the consensus necessary for a wise decision.

It is very important to be sure that decision making is the ultimate outcome. Telling people in advance that conclusions are the purpose and then conducting an information session may communicate to participants that their input isn't really important or that the rule of thumb at your institution is that people meet and meet but nothing gets decided.

If a group gets stuck, a leader can break the impasse by summarizing what has been agreed upon and what remains undecided. Should the members remain stuck, they may grant the leader the decision-making prerogative in the interest of moving forward.

Idea Development

Known popularly as brainstorming, this group purpose assumes that several heads are better than none. Freewheeling sessions can lead to ideas that wouldn't have come up in isolation or to improvements on existing ideas. Leaders need to set the tone for this purpose by remaining open to any suggestion or proposal. If participants don't feel safe enough to throw their ideas into the pot, this can be a useless activity. Leaders must also avoid evaluating each new idea as it arises. Quick judgments discourage others from taking the risk of making suggestions.

Resolving Differences

A brewing conflict within a group will continue to fester and grow unless it is exposed to the light of day. This is best accomplished in a group session where participants can hear all sides of the issue. Naturally, leaders need to have solid conflict management skills before attempting to accomplish this purpose (see the section on "dealing with conflict" in chapter 3). Otherwise, the situation is very likely to get worse rather than better.

Reaching Acceptance

Even though a decision has been made through consensus, there may still be lingering doubts or resentment. Here the leader may call a meeting to reiterate the reasons for the decision and discuss the consequences. At no time would the leader suggest that the decision could be altered. Rather, this is a time to air concerns so that the institution can move forward.

There are two attributes of a good decision that are critical to reaching acceptance. It must have quality—it's the right thing to do given the current situation, and legitimacy—it must be reached with the endorsement of key members of the institution.

GROUP SIZE

The group's size is a strong factor influencing the success or failure of achieving its purpose. Too large and the group becomes unmanageable; too small and it may not be perceived as legitimate.

The strong tendency is toward groups that are too large. One university I know about had a tradition of bringing key administrators together for a working retreat in August, just before the academic year began. The event was desirable, in part, because it took place at a posh lakeside estate. More important, though, was the panache an invitation carried with it. Being included made one important; thus "seats" at this event were hot-ticket items. Soon more people were included, then still more the next year, and so on until the practicality of the meeting was entirely lost since almost no decisions could be reached. And, of course, the cost of the retreat went out of control.

A good guideline is the *principle of least group size*. Groups must be large enough to include people with the skills necessary to arrive at a good decision, but no larger. Now, that may mean a comparatively large group is assembled, if it is determined that each person involved is needed for his or her skills, knowledge, and/or influence.

Using the Goldilocks model, there are some groups—two to four people—that can be too small for the purpose. Assertive participants tend to run the show, intimidating the less talkative members who might feel more comfortable with more people around. There are groups that are too large. These can be both necessary and managed effectively, but the leader must assume far greater responsibility for making sure the group's purpose is achieved in the time allotted. I will offer some suggestions for working with groups of 40 or more later on, though I don't recommend this activity to leaders just starting out.

I have found that a membership of five to nine people is just about right. This group is more comfortable for the shy, more likely to represent diverse views, and more able to come to a good decision. A large group can be broken into clusters of five to nine members to work on a part of the purpose. When all participants reconvene, the smaller groups' suggestions will have greater quality and legitimacy than would otherwise be the case.

GROUP FUNCTIONS

Regardless of their purpose or size, groups can serve one of two primary functions: accomplishing a task or meeting social/emotional needs. I contend that most groups serve both, though in an organization such as a college or university the task function should always lead.

Social and Emotional Needs

Groups meet social and emotional needs through the human interaction that takes place primarily before and after the agenda of a meeting begins, but also during the meeting itself. Unfortunately, these legitimate functions can supersede the work that must be done throughout the meeting. Leaders need to be cognizant of this function, respect it, and help to channel it appropriately.

One of the best ways to do that is to welcome a certain amount of socializing. Have refreshments available if that's appropriate. Plan for a coffee break. Encourage discussions about the group's work to continue over lunch. Make jokes, especially at your expense. The lighter parts of the meeting help groups come together, gain greater cohesiveness, and relieve some of the tension that may be present.

Beware of straying too far into the fun and games. Even the most light-hearted of the participants knows that work is the purpose of an institutional meeting. If nothing ever gets done, people will legitimately surmise that their time is being wasted.

Task Function

The task function is, of course, what everyone identifies as the purpose of the group. Finishing a project, making decisions, stimulating new ideas, and reviewing job candidates are clear mandates. And the leader is responsible ultimately for staying on target. However, leaders can be too task-oriented and find themselves stifling innovative thinking or ignoring important morale-building opportunities.

A group that is all business, though, and never acknowledges the human factor can quickly fall apart under pressure. That's because the members have no loyalty to one another and no group cohesion. Why go out on a limb or work hard under these conditions?

I believe that a 70-30 task/social needs split is healthy. If 70 percent of the group's time is spent on the job at hand, leaders can relax. Then there will be ample time to honor birthdays, new babies, and outstanding achievements, and to express group sympathy for colleagues' times of trouble such as a death in the family.

While there is no hard and fast rule for dividing a group's time into the two functions, I believe leaders can develop a sensitivity that will tell them when to shift from one to the other. Expressions of frustration that the job isn't getting done mean it's time to get down to business; excessive watch monitoring, glazed eyes, and generalized restlessness may signal that it's time for a break.

GROUP SKILLS

I assume that, by now, you understand that working with groups of people is part of the operative definition of leadership. And, while most people who want to lead genuinely like other human beings, most leaders have inadequate and underdeveloped group skills. It's as if we expect our leaders to intuitively figure out how to handle group situations. I don't. I expect leaders to work on their skills continually. The following are some areas to explore that apply to small groups.

Know and Employ Positive Group Behaviors

1. Initiating. The group begins its work through activities such as defining the problem or suggesting a process for accomplishing the tasks at hand. The leader assumes responsibility for fielding ideas and consolidating them in a list so the group can agree on the best definition or procedure.

2. Information seeking. Members of the group ask each other questions to gather the facts, data, and opinions necessary to accomplish their work. This process not only clarifies issues (and most people have only a partial understanding of these, whether they admit or not), it encourages greater participation. The leader can help this happen by asking specific members to respond to questions, especially those who may be reluctant to join in out of shyness. The caution here is to avoid a free-for-all in which many opinions, but very few facts, are aired.

3. Summarizing. The leader or another participant restates what the group has accomplished to check for accuracy and understanding. The goal is to tease out any missing information and air any simmering disagreements that could stall progress later on. The end product of an effective summary is closure, that point from which the group can move forward to the next set of tasks.

4. Standard setting. Closely allied with summarizing is reaching consensus on the standards for this particular group. These can include the number of meetings, the method by which information will be shared (meeting notes, new information, etc.), the number and types of subcommittees, the expected date for completion, and a frank appraisal of the group's progress.

The leader should foster positive group roles—not only ensuring they are acted out, but also enforcing and rewarding their implementation. This is best accomplished by expressing appreciation, pointing out successes, and serving as a consistent role model.

Know and Discourage Negative Group Behaviors

Leaders need to be familiar with the conscious or unconscious behaviors that can halt forward progress for a group. Once identified, of course, these behaviors must be gently but firmly addressed, which is often difficult for a leader and others to do while remaining sensitive to group morale and individual needs.

1. Aggression: personal attacks, belittling others' ideas, expressing overt hostility

2. Grandstanding: boasting of personal achievements, claiming another's idea as one's own

3. Dominating: interrupting, manipulating the discussion, using humiliation or flattery of others as a means of taking control

4. Blocking: negativism or resistance beyond the bounds of reason, persisting in a discussion when the rest of the group has come to consensus.

5. Goofing off: playing the clown, remaining detached, carrying on side conversations, consistently tardy

6. Approval seeking: playing on the sympathy of the group by self-depreciation, continually looking to the leader for validation of one's ideas and contributions

It's clear that good leaders need to deal with these behaviors right away or they can bring forward motion to a screeching halt. At the very least, they waste valuable time and resources while stretching group members' patience to the limit. Naturally, leaders need to steer clear of personal attacks or humiliation as techniques to redirect the group's energies to a more productive tack. But there are ways and times that are appropriate for addressing negative behaviors.

During the summary period, the leader can address some concerns. Comments like, "During this session, we seem to have given too much time to fun and games. I don't mind that once in a while, but I know we all want to finish by our agreed-upon deadline." Or "I'd like to see everyone join in the discussion next time. This is, after all, a group project, and I don't think we've tapped everyone's good ideas yet." Or "Let's keep in mind next time the need to avoid making comments personal. That never seems to help and I really want to avoid hurt feelings."

The next time a negative behavior surfaces the leader can act right away. For instance, a personal attack can be nipped in mid-sentence with a gentle but firm reminder to stick to the task. The goof-off who attempts to distract can be ignored and a determined blocker can be directed to the next task rather than given more time to air complaints.

If a problem persists, the leader should meet with the offending party privately. It's more likely that a concern will be aired in the safer environment of a one-to-one discussion if the leader is careful to give the person ample chance to speak his or her piece. If all else fails, a member whose behavior continues to inhibit group progress must be removed or isolated.

Keys to Running an Effective Meeting

One of the reasons most people greet the prospect of a meeting with groans is that they are so often poorly run. They start late, materials and information aren't available, the agenda is nonexistent or never followed, ramblers and complainers are allowed to ramble and complain ad nauseum, and no one leaves the room with a sense of accomplishment. No wonder meetings are great opportunities to improve doodling skills, wool-gather, or mentally write the grocery list.

At one university system, the cry went out loud and clear—"We have too many meetings to attend!!" A survey indicated that there were more than 200 system meetings annually involving thousands of people for thousands of hours. A questionnaire supplied the information to make a few refinements, eliminate a few meetings, and turn others into teleconferences.

But the most productive outcome was a guide for greater effectiveness developed for deans, directors, and other administrators. Once followed, these suggestions helped make many meetings much more effective.

Preparation

Define the general purpose of this specific meeting. Is it to make an announcement and take questions about a reorganization? Is it to come up with improvements for recruiting students? Is it to resolve an ongoing conflict?

Set clear goals for the meeting. Once the announcement is made, do you hope to reach a decision or help group members accept the news? With new ideas for recruiting, how will they be implemented?

With the first two questions answered, ask another, harder one. Is the meeting really necessary? Perhaps it is possible to meet the goals without a formal gathering. Maybe the time isn't quite ripe for a decision. It could be a good time for the meeting, but the key participants are not available. A teleconference or a questionnaire might suffice.

Communication

Gather and send all necessary materials to participants in advance. (A week ahead is usually sufficient. Send it too soon and participants will forget the information. Send it too late, and participants will complain they didn't have enough time.)

At minimum, the materials should spell out the purpose and goals of the meeting. An itemized agenda listing times allotted and presenters of the topics is very helpful. A statement or two about the desired outcomes will focus attention on the tasks at hand far more than an open-ended approach.

Meeting

Start on time. Leave no more than five minutes for latecomers and insist that breaks begin and end on schedule. A willingness to wait for stragglers punishes the conscientious members and destroys group cohesion. And waiting for latecomers can redefine the "real" meeting time from 9:00 A.M., say, to 9:30 next time, to 9:45, and so on.

Begin by stating the purpose of the meeting, the goals to be achieved, and the desired outcomes. If there are formal minutes to approve, do so, but don't revisit the issues covered.

Stick to the agenda, but don't be unnecessarily rigid. If it makes sense to cover an item after, rather than before, the break, then do that for the sake of the group's morale. It's usually good strategy to deal with one or two easy issues first. The group can feel successful as it moves on to more complicated matters. And don't try to cover too much. That can lead to rushing through the meeting.

Provide a brief history of each issue as you go along. Don't assume everyone there is at the same level of understanding. Suggest a range of possible solutions and remind the group of any constraints, budgetary or otherwise.

By employing the group skills listed above—information seeking, initiating, standard setting, and so on—keep the group moving forward. As leader, you are responsible for the pace and must keep foot-dragging or rushes to judgment to a minimum.

Allow ample time for summarizing. Recapitulate decisions, itemize conclusions, and clarify assignments. Finally, critique the meeting, praising successful efforts and suggesting improvements for the next session.

Decision Making in Larger Groups

If, in spite of operating by the principle of least size, you must work with a medium- to large-sized group (between 20 and 100 people), you will need some specific techniques to arrive at decisions. Without the ease and intimacy of a group of five to nine people, the larger groups can become mired in details or tangled in high emotion quite quickly. As a leader, you need to be able to move beyond this morass and on to reaching the goals you've set.

Two techniques suggest themselves immediately:

- Majority rule. Adopted by most legislatures, decisions are made by the majority. Often this technique is effective, especially if the vote is heavily in favor or opposed. But when votes split 55-45, there is a risk that a proposal, even though adopted, will never be implemented. At the least, the sizable minority may feel left out and resentful, a good breeding ground for resistance next time. In most situations, greater acceptance by a group is both desirable and reachable.
- Complete agreement. The Society of Friends (known popularly as the Quakers) will keep meeting until every member agrees with a decision. Those who oppose are asked for concessions, as is the rest of the group, but there is no forward movement until all are on

board. Certainly this contributes greatly to group cohesion. But keep in mind that Friends form tight-knit, long-term communities, so this process doesn't take as long as you might suppose. Most other groups don't have this luxury and thus can't hope for 100 percent agreement every time.

Fortunately there are more effective, less time-consuming methods for reaching decisions.

Consensus Seeking

Consensus is as much a feeling as a fact in the group process. As you become a more seasoned leader, you will begin to sense that the membership is coalescing around a decision and that those who have reservations have become more willing to buy in. Nevertheless, following a procedure is always important.

Begin by following the planning and communication strategies discussed above. Once the issue is clearly stated and understood, encourage the group to suggest alternative decisions. List and discuss the alternatives by soliciting support or opposition for each. Make certain that a specific opinion is expressed just once rather than several times in different words (which is deadly in a larger group).

Take a straw vote. If a clear consensus emerges (70 percent or more in favor or against), move on to the next issue and start the process again. If no clear consensus appears, seek modifications or concessions. Then take another straw vote. If a decision is still not forthcoming, tabling and moving on may be appropriate.

At the meeting's conclusion, summarize the decisions reached. Ask for a vote on the entire package. Remember you're not just seeking decisions; you want support for these decisions. Only then will implementation be successful.

In spite of your best efforts, consensus may still elude the group. Still, you've encouraged and supported full participation. Perhaps next time this group can make further progress.

Nominal Groups

Nominal groups are useful when the opinions of a large number of people are necessary before a decision can be made. Work is accomplished without the group actually meeting or, if the group does meet, there is little interaction.

A nominal group could be asked to generate ideas by electronic mail or by writing them down at a meeting to be collected and tallied later. In a nominal group session, the leader defines the issue and asks for solutions. He or she then systematically polls the room by asking each member to state an idea, one person at a time. Once these are listed (and similar ideas are collapsed together for simplicity), there may or may not be a brief discussion for clarification purposes. Then the leader asks each group member to write down his or her ranking order of preference. These are collected and tallied.

At this point, some alternatives will wither for lack of support. Others will form a top three or top five. A brief discussion will isolate the pros and cons of each of the remaining suggestions. A final vote can then be taken to reach a conclusion.

Consensus seeking and nominal groups minimize wasting time and maximize participation in larger groups. Still, the solutions reached may not be fully fleshed out. Or there may be lingering doubts. If so, break up the group into cells of five to seven people and assign a consensus-seeking exercise to each.

Here's how I've seen it work. A university president-elect, in his desire to get a jump start on his new administration, asked that a group of 100 faculty, staff, and student leaders be assembled prior to his arrival. In groups of eight or nine, they were to identify the most pressing issues facing the institution. That data was gathered, compiled, and mailed to each participant. Each selected the top 10 issues, as he or she saw it. This information was tabulated and sent to the president.

Once on campus, the president and his key administrators met with the group of 100. Again they split into groups of eight or nine with the task of selecting the top three issues from the original 10, a process that took about two hours. Reassembled into one room, the smaller groups each presented their choices. Consensus was reached very swiftly at that point with the top five issues emerging as overwhelming favorites.

Certainly this was a valuable exercise for everyone and yielded benefits for all; it was especially helpful for the new president. In a very short time he had consensus on the major issues facing the institution, a common acceptance of those issues, and a platform on which he could build for the early months of his tenure.

Fostering Creativity

Groups can be very creative, even more creative than individuals. Members encourage others to suggest still more. That will happen when members feel that it is safe and appropriate to give voice to their imagination.

Unfortunately, too often "group-think" conformity is rewarded. Leaders who want new ideas, new solutions, and new directions will have to help the group think outside the lines.

First, *ban judgments.* Let the ideas flow freely, the wilder and more imaginative the better. Withhold evaluation, the universal wet blanket for creativity. This isn't easy. Educated people are taught to evaluate and assess, not create.

Second, *set no limits.* Today's oddball idea could be tomorrow's breakthrough.

Third, *go for quantity.* The first 10 ideas are just a warm-up. Once the floodgates open, many more possibilities will show up. It's far easier to pick 10 good ideas from 100 than one good idea from 10.

Don't permit selling or lengthy explanations. Like trying to explain why you love someone, good things sometimes need expression, not edification.

Encourage full participation. The quieter types may harbor the best ideas of all. Once the group is warmed up and producing, call on the nonparticipants by name. They may just be waiting for an opening to join in.

Record all ideas. At the end of the session, organize ideas into categories and collapse similar ones. If necessary, divide the group into cells for discussion. Or use the nominal group technique to determine the group's top choices.

Finally, *take a vote and then summarize the results.*

I've seen this process generate as many as 30 new ideas in less than half an hour. A recent session I heard about involved 15 faculty and staff members charged with improving the student recruitment process. Once the 30 ideas were put forth, a discussion limited to an hour ensued in which the person whose idea was "up" elaborated. Other members served as devil's advocates.

Then the group selected by consensus the 10 most viable ideas. A subsequent session was devoted to suggestions for implementing these improvements and resulted in a solid, workable plan.

Interpersonal and group skills will take you far. In fact, no leader can succeed without them. Bumble along, yes. Succeed, no.

You also need skills and understandings specific to your being effective with the social institution you've inherited. In the last analysis, personal and group skills will help you get the job as leader. Doing that job requires an understanding of social institutions, how they change, how they deal with grief, and how you can be a part of their transformation into something even better. Those are the topics of the next chapter.

CHAPTER 5

Transforming Organizations

Progress is a nice word. But change is its motivator. And change has its enemies.

—Robert Kennedy

LEADING TOWARD RENEWAL

For most organizations, the guiding rule seems to be that nothing new should happen here for the first time. Change is an anathema, even when members are in full cry that the state of affairs couldn't be worse and that morale is at an all-time low.

Of course, stability isn't a bad thing. In fact, most organizations thrive on continuity since it enables its members to pass through times of stress, secure in the knowledge that crises will be met rationally, fairly, efficiently, and in accordance with tradition. Max Weber called this the principle of legal rationality.

Known more familiarly, this principle translates as "the way things are done around here." And it is good to know that certain things will happen in just about the same way each time—that a university commencement will include its particular pomp and circumstance or that a board of directors will suspend meetings during the summer months or even that the football team will always have a bad season.

Preserving the status quo does have its downside, of course. An organization bound by tradition is almost never ready to react to and cope with change from the outside.

And, of course, change will come, like it or not. It seems that with each year the pace of change accelerates. Dial phones give way to push-button phones that give way to cordless phones that yield to cellular phones. Lumbering mainframe computers yield to PCs connected by servers that open the way to the mysteries of the Internet. Medical science moves from palliative care to miracles that push the boundaries of life and death. Local economies are inextricably entwined with the national economy, which in turn moves to a global rhythm. Jobs that often lasted a working lifetime have become way stations in people's lives as they move from one career to the next.

Any organization that refuses to acknowledge this fact of modern life and make itself ready to adapt is doomed to inevitable obscurity. Leaders, especially, must be in the vanguard encouraging, nudging, supporting, and even prodding others to make changes as necessary.

Naturally, leaders come to their positions with new ideas in mind. Often they are appointed or elected because they are creative and have a fresh perspective. However, most leaders are more innovators than they are inventors.

Inventors generate new ideas. Innovators sift through new ideas, select the best ones, and then help the organization implement them. There is usually no shortage of ideas, especially if a leader supports creative thinking and freewheeling discussions. Putting these good ideas into place is another matter, since new ideas naturally lead to change. And, as I've said, change— even positive change—is difficult.

What, then, can a leader do to ease the way toward change? The first step is a personal inventory.

Taking a Personal Inventory

Are you committed to continual self-renewal? It is not enough to be a champion of change; you must be willing to change yourself as needed. If you stick rigidly to business as usual, rarely try new approaches, and fail in other ways to set an example, you cannot expect your organization to take the risks that are part of true innovation.

Defending Your Organization

Do you serve as the chief defender of your organization? Members of your organization must trust that you will support it through thick and thin. If you are frequently critical of the organization, people will come to believe that they have been doing a poor job and have far less motivation to try harder. First, leaders need to sing the praises of the fine work the organization has been doing. Then, they can help others move toward improving what is already good.

This is called "building up idiosyncrasy credits." Members of the organization implicitly tell the leader to "first subscribe to our norms and help us achieve our goals; then we'll work with you to advance positive change." Smart leaders, then, embrace the values, mission, and vision of the organization and seize opportunities to point out how members are already achieving. Constituents are asking for proof that the leader is really one of them. Leaders must show that they are.

Most of us have seen this theory proved in the negative. Some leaders come into their positions believing they have a mandate to institute wholesale change as soon as possible. They run roughshod over the staff, are openly critical in public, and have a long list of the reasons why the organization is failing. Such a leader rarely has a long tenure. The colleagues will see to that, as well they should.

Creating a Fertile Environment for Change

Do you know how to create a fertile environment for change? The following elements are necessary:

1. Widespread understanding and support for the organization's mission and vision. It's very hard to move forward if you don't know where you are. As leader, you need to be able to articulate the reason why the organization exists as simply and as often as possible. When the mission and vision become a visible part of the culture, deciding what needs to be done to move forward becomes easier.
2. A spirit of openness. Have the confidence to be candid. Let members of the organization know the truth, even when that might be painful. Only when everyone is on the same page can you move toward change.
3. An invitation to participate. People need to feel involved. Time taken up front to bring people up to speed will pay off later. Those with the greatest motivation to sabotage growth are those who feel they have been ignored.
4. Continuing reassurances. People on the brink of change feel very vulnerable. They need and deserve to hear that they are on the right track. A good leader offers this kind of support frequently along with information and opportunities to discuss feelings and concerns.

5. Sufficient preparation for those charged with implementing change. Resistance is often born out of fear that we are not up to the current challenge. Provide training, skill development, consultants, and other support as appropriate, and people will nearly always respond positively.

6. A reward system. We all know that positive reinforcement is more effective than punishment. But too often organizations are quicker to blame than to praise. Be certain that successes are recognized with public fanfare whenever possible. Rewards can be monetary, but not necessarily. Recognition by a personal note, a paragraph in a newsletter, or a round of applause are also well received. (See the section on motivation in chapter 3.)

7. Infrequent failures. While accepting mistakes without shaming or punishment is essential in a climate of renewal, frequent failures will lead to overwhelming frustrations. Sometimes it's better to try an experimental program rather than a wholesale change. The willingness to innovate in a small way steers clear of the "all or nothing" thinking that can stifle creative approaches.

Leaders are the keepers of the climate of renewal. While you won't be working to implement improvements all by yourself, you are the head cheerleader whose optimism is critical. If your positive outlook flags during the inevitable setbacks, focus on longer term progress. Are things better today than they were a year ago? six months ago? If they are, renew your energy from these successes. If not, revisit the plan with your organization for fine tuning.

One public institution found itself caught in a vise of conflicting state priorities and a finite state budget. The demand for funding for health care, welfare, and elementary and secondary education was growing, shunting higher education into fourth or fifth place in priority.

With no increase in the budget and a small decrease in new student applications, the state university was in a major funk. The president had to do something to lure people out of the ongoing self-pity festival on campus.

She brought representatives together to seek consensus on the major issues facing the university. From these, several "low-hanging apples" were selected. These were the issues that could be handled quickly with every reason to expect success.

Soon there were measurable improvements in parking, benefits, and operating budgets—not major changes, but they were crowd pleasers and important steps in the right direction. More complex budget issues were handed to a strategic planning task force. Another group made up largely of faculty tackled curriculum improvements. In both cases, experimental programs were spun off quickly to test some alternatives. Finally, an innovation fund was developed to spur academic improvements.

Now just about everyone on campus was involved in change. All the while, the president served as the state university's prime advocate. She acknowledged the depths of the challenges but took every chance she could to remind people that they could prevail if they worked together. Sometimes her energy flagged and her hopes diminished, but she never revealed those feelings to the community.

The result was a university that had begun to embrace change as the appropriate answer to its challenges.

ORGANIZATIONAL GRIEF

Change always requires us to let go of a piece of the past. This process may be as benign as updating the university mascot. Or it may be truly traumatic, such as the wholesale restructuring of an organization requiring significant staff layoffs. In either case, the wise leader allows for a natural process of grieving to take place.

When the change is of large proportion, stress, frustration, fear, and anger are normal feelings. And leaders often bear the brunt of all this pain. There is some comfort from knowing that difficulties can strengthen an organization and that the acrimony directed toward you isn't really about you but rather the loss of equilibrium people are experiencing. Philosophers and poets remind us that that which does not destroy us will make us stronger. Still, the grieving process requires both courage and persistence.

The Stages of Grief

The stages of grief have been defined by Elisabeth Kubler-Ross and others.[1] Most often they are associated with an individual, especially a person who is facing imminent death. Groups, though, even very large ones such as major businesses and institutions go through a very similar process.

1. Denial. Refusing to deal with reality is often a necessary buffer for people. It gives them time to absorb the truth internally and to avoid overreacting to bad news. Denial can lead to strange behavior, though. As the leader of more than one higher education institution, I've

devoted a great deal of time to informing others about a crisis at hand only to be told later that I have been keeping people in the dark. Even when organization members do grasp the problem, they often resort to simplistic solutions as they stall for time to absorb the complexities of their current situation and continue to hope that the problems will disappear.

2. Anger. A good defense against feelings of sadness and vulnerability is anger. The defiance and righteous indignation that attend bad news are normal, though often difficult for leaders to accept. Expect that others will talk behind your back and even go so far as to take a vote of no confidence. As long as these feelings do not become destructive, they should be respected in the short term. Of course, it's important not to get stuck in this phase, since anger can become a very destructive force.

3. Bargaining. As members of the organization attempt to postpone the inevitable, they promise to be "good." They'll work longer hours, brainstorm solutions, and raise more money if only the bad news will go away. Bargaining is denial with an agenda.

4. Depression. Finally the organization gives up its attempts to push the truth away. This is a bleak time for most since it seems that there is no light at the end of the tunnel. Depression in this context is both a reaction to the situation and a step in the preparation for accepting loss. Loss is, after all, a very painful thing. Sadness and gloom are natural reactions.

5. Acceptance. At first, accepting loss seems to be the absence of feeling as members of the organization become stoic in the face of reality. But gradually acceptance becomes hope as renewal leads the way to growth and positive change.

As helpful as these descriptions are, it's important to note that the process of grieving is rarely entirely linear. Some steps are skipped to be revisited later. Others can dominate for longer periods of time. Leaders are well advised to understand this process, allow themselves to experience it, and sensitively and firmly help others do the same.

Leadership Strategies for Organizational Grief

Accepting grieving as a normal process accomplishes three important things for leaders. First, it enables them to help others understand what is going on and therefore move toward acceptance more rapidly. Second, it helps leaders deal with the anger directed toward them without taking it personally. And third, it makes it easier for the organization if the leader gives due attention to emotional aspects of change rather than retreating to the safety of strictly rational approaches.

The following sections are some effective techniques for dealing with the stages of organizational grief.

Repetition

It's estimated that people need to hear a message 28 times before they internalize it. Meet denial by gently but firmly repeating and reinforcing the truth. Make use of meetings, publications, public events, and other communication outlets as opportunities to outline the situation and restate the reasons for hope. Be certain that key members of the organization have the information they need and the support they need to serve as spokespersons as well. Enlist the assistance of leaders of other organizations and consultants who have the luxury of illuminating the truth and then escaping before denial turns to anger.

Personal Detachment

When the anger surfaces, detach from it even as you accept it. Concentrate on the reality of the situation and the hope for the future and avoid entirely returning the anger with your own. At the same time, it's important to stay close to the organization and its members. It may be very tempting to head to higher ground during periods of great stress, but a leader's visibility is critically important at these times.

Optimism

Organization-wide depression is best countered with solidly grounded optimism. When members express the belief that things will never get any better, the leader's job is to convince them they're wrong. While words of encouragement are very helpful, actions are even better. This might be a great time to publicly reward people for outstanding work, introduce a family-friendly program like flex-time, or host an all-staff party. The point is to keep things moving by involving people fully in the process of renewal.

Timing

Stay close to the organization so you can act immediately when acceptance becomes widespread. At no time will the organization be more receptive to forward progress than now. They've stopped hoping for the good old days to return. Now they're ready to take hold of the vision for the future.

THE MOMENT OF TRUTH

No longer stuck in the grieving process, the organization is ready to deal directly with its unique problems and solutions. A good leader is also ready with a plan and a process.

Defining the Problem

It's important for everyone to buy into the definition of the challenge. In higher education, for example, the problem in the late 1980s and early 1990s was a demographic dip in the number of college-aged men and women, plus an uncertain economy. This, in turn, led to an inevitable diminution of demand for college and university services, necessitating immediate action.

It was apparent to most that services would need to be cut or reduced, with an inescapable reduction in the workforce. This was a bitter truth, but one that had to be faced.

Gathering and Sharing Information

In keeping with the spirit of openness described above, leaders are well advised to provide accurate data to give shape to the problem. People need a clear picture of what the resources are and what deficits are expected. When possible, members of the organization can be invited to participate in defining solutions, with their leaders gently but firmly keeping them based in the reality of the situation.

Seeking Advice

Reach out to the membership in an organized fashion. Actively solicit opinions, suggestions, and solutions in a variety of ways. For small organizations, this can take the form of a series of meetings for everyone. For larger ones, advice can be solicited in written form to be commented on in various forums, focus groups, or task forces. (The group skills discussed in chapter 4 are particularly helpful.)

If feasible, outside consultants can be very helpful. Their distance from the organization, combined with their expertise, can offer an entirely new perspective on problems.

Focusing on the Mission

Be certain that, in their zeal to make changes, members of your organization do not stray from the mission, vision, and values that you, as leader, have reinforced and reiterated whenever possible. Each suggestion must be measured against its potential to strengthen the core of the organization. Some ideas, no matter how creative, may have to be rejected because they do not contribute to the mission.

Implementing Changes

It seems an obvious step, but many organizations falter at this point. The enthusiasm generated by the renewal and restructuring process can come to seem like change itself. But concrete plans enacted as promised are the end point of the process, and good leaders see to it that this happens.

WORKING WITH YOUR TEAM

Leaders who expect to devote most of their energies to thinking great thoughts and expounding upon them while the organization hums like a well-oiled machine are doomed to disappointment. In fact, the majority of your time will be spent working with teams. And the greater portion of that time will be spent with your own management team.

Once again, balance is important. Spend too little time managing your team and you'll be putting out fires all too frequently. Spend too much time managing people and you won't fulfill your role as the chief advocate for the institution's mission and vision.

I have found that working with a team of five to 10 people who report directly to me is best. This way I can provide adequate supervision, have a good idea about what is going on in the organization, and tend to the leadership responsibilities that are mine alone to carry out.

In fact, the smaller number of direct reports is so important that I suggest you conduct an institutional analysis and a self-analysis to discover why a larger group must have your attention. Is it a fact of life at that particular institution or the result of poor management by your predecessor? Is it an unnecessary ego involvement on your part? Examine the situation, but make an effort to work with the smaller number of individuals.

As you work with your team, make certain that each team member *supports the goals of the organization.* Give them time to argue a different perspective if necessary. But when consensus has been reached or when negotiations have struck a workable compromise, all team members must adhere to the current plan.

Those who cannot support the goals can be invited to resign. Failure to work in concert with the leader and with the rest of the team is insubordination, plain and simple. Nothing will drain your energy faster and slow down progress more than a senior staff member bent on his or her own agenda.

Once your team is with you, you can reinforce the importance of mission, vision, and goals by asking each member to draw up similar statements for their own areas. These statements should have a direct relationship to the organization's plans, of course. They can also be a useful tool to measure progress as time goes along.

Allow your team the freedom to do the work they have been given by *delegating both authority and responsibility.* By delegating, your team will know you have faith in their abilities. They will also know, as they should, that they are fully accountable for their areas. If you find yourself doing someone else's work, countermanding their decisions, or correcting sloppy work, one of you is in the wrong position.

It's true that many people will want to present their problems to you rather than to someone further down the line. After all, having the leader's ear is a mark of status. But you are mistaken if you give in to such flattery. You must redirect concerns to the person responsible whenever possible (which should be most of the time). The exception comes when someone wants to praise a team member for outstanding work. You should pass the word on, but you can keep some for yourself since you showed great foresight in hiring this stellar performer.

Make certain that your team has all the information they need. In my experience, few things are worth keeping secret. As leader, you are the primary conduit for information. Make certain that news, policy changes, budget facts, and the like are distributed regularly. Have regular meetings with your team. These should be command performances, excused only for reasons of plague or pestilence. Use electronic mail. Take advantage of new mechanisms as they come along. But keep in mind that your team is only as effective as the information they have to work with, and they will get that primarily from you.

Finally, *support your team.* These people work hard for you and with you. They deserve your loyalty. When they make mistakes, be forgiving. Give genuine praise as often as you can. And stand by them publicly, especially when the heat is on.

Hiring New Team Members

More often than not, new leaders inherit a team when they take office. Over time, though, vacancies will occur, giving you an opportunity to bring someone on board to help further the organization's goals. When this opportunity presents itself, be sure to give yourself enough time to ensure a good fit between person and job.

Think about your own strengths and weaknesses and those of the rest of the team. What do you need? More creativity? More organization? More human resource sense? Finding complementary skills in a new hire isn't easy, particularly since, left to our own devices, we will seek someone very much like ourselves. It's important to put aside the comfort factor in the best interests of the organization.

Techniques for Interviewing

There are several good techniques for interviewing. I like grouping questions into three categories, each of which will elicit important information.

1. Thinking questions. Ask the candidate what she or he thinks about certain issues central to your organization's mission, such as, "What do you think about distance education? the future of tenure? multiculturalism?" Here you will discover not only how well versed the candidate is on the issues, but also how well she or he can put her or his thoughts into understandable, persuasive words.

2. Problem questions. Ask what the candidate sees as the major problems, contentions, or roadblocks inherent in the issues you raised in the first set of questions, such as, "What is the downside of distance education? abolishing tenure? requiring a course in multiculturalism of all undergraduates?" Being able to detect the thorns shows that a candidate has thought about these issues and knows that one solution will not meet all needs.

3. Implementation questions. Toughest of all and where most searches falter, these questions aim for the candidate's ability to move from idea to action, such as, "How would you help the institution enter the distance education market? deal with retrenchment? institute a new requirement in the curriculum?"

Naturally, no candidate will possess outstanding strengths in every area (if she or he does, watch out—she or he may soon have your job!). Nevertheless, with the goal of balance for the team in mind, you'll have a good idea whether this candidate would be a good complement as well as a contributor to the well-being of the organization.

Sometimes leaders have a hard time balancing a team. A colleague readily admitted that she had difficulty getting her mind around the intricacies of the budget, especially in the area of strategic planning. Yet she couldn't seem to warm up to the hard-headed budget people who traditionally hold these positions, so there wasn't one on her team. But then a major fiscal crisis hit and her team was crippled by this omission.

Too often, we are impressed by rhetoric and forget about the harder slog of turning plans into reality. An adept job candidate can sway a search committee with his or her impassioned vision and deep commitment to the cause. Don't forget to ask about implementation skills. Ask him or her in the interviews, and ask his or her references.

USING LEADERSHIP MUSCLE

Improving Quality

As good as the team approach is, there are times when nothing less than a full-court press, personal endorsement, and ongoing support from the leader of a higher education institution will do. This is especially true when something quite new makes its debut on campus.

At the risk of overemphasizing a point, I say again that leadership in an organization steeped in tradition is different. Like the church, higher education has held itself apart from the grittier life "out there." Until just recently, this exemption has been reinforced by people in and outside of colleges and universities. Thus, innovations that have worked well in the marketplace tend to meet stiff resistance inside the academy.

Quality improvement initiatives are a case in point. When one such method was introduced on my campus a few years ago, it didn't exactly meet a chorus of approval. For many, a new way of working felt like a negative assessment of the work they had been doing all along. For others, the approach seemed like a way to get people to do more work at a time when layoffs were happening. And for others, the notion of students as "customers" was hard to accept.

But I had seen the method work at other higher education institutions, and I knew it could here under the right conditions. And it was important to me for two reasons: (1) We needed to increase the efficiency and cost-effectiveness of our services in the wake of a major restructuring, and (2) we needed a way to help people feel they were really making a difference for the primary consumers at our institution—the students.

We elected a gradual approach to implementing the program rather than a total immersion. This saved some money, of course. But more important, the step-by-step method allowed for some early successes that could be publicized as illustrations for the rest of the campus that this effort could work.

Syracuse University Improving Quality

The first to be trained in what became Syracuse University Improving Quality (SUIQ) were the six members of my administrative cabinet. We then designed and implemented a pilot program for several key impact areas such as the bursar's office, the financial aid office, health services, and classroom environments. Based on their results (which were impressive for something as new as this was), the training program began in earnest for the nearly 3,000 administrative and academic support staff, with a training process that took more than two years to complete.

In the simplest terms, SUIQ means meeting the customer's needs by understanding what they are, determining what should be done differently as a result of that understanding, making the appropriate changes, and then measuring progress toward meeting the needs.

Of course, SUIQ has required a great deal of time and effort. Thousands of hours have been devoted to training. Many hundreds of hours have gone to the extra work that goes into any attempt to do things differently.

It has also required ongoing support from the top. Accordingly, I have served as the director of a steering committee representative of every aspect of campus life. Members of that committee make annual reports about the progress of SUIQ in their areas. From these reports come information that is used in my speeches, on a regular page in the campus newspaper that highlights successes, and in a monthly newsletter that serves as my vehicle to comment on the initiative's wisdom and warts.

The latter is known as *BuzzWords* (see examples in appendix A), which has become a widely read vehicle that elicits comments—not always positive, to be sure—from internal and external constituencies (the latter is a result of its presence on the World Wide Web). Keeping the goal of continuous improvement in the forefront, *BuzzWords* is serving an important purpose. It does so by demonstrating my ongoing commitment to SUIQ, without which its chances of success are considerably reduced.

So far I've been making the case that personal and group skills are essential to effective leadership. Also critical is understanding how social institutions work.

But there is another constituency—your external public—that matters very much. It's important to look and act the part of a leader. The next chapter takes a look at these skills.

NOTE

1.   Elisabeth Kubler-Ross, *On Death and Dying,* New York: Macmillan, 1969.

CHAPTER 6

Dealing with the Public

In old days [people] had the rack. Now they have the press.
— Oscar Wilde

Philanthropy is the refuge of people who wish to annoy their fellow creatures.
— Oscar Wilde

A speaker with a national reputation for anti-semitism is due on campus tomorrow at the invitation of one of your student groups.

Students, on a lark, have burglarized a mausoleum near one of the residence halls and are discovered because of the stench coming from their room as they boil a human skull over a hotplate.

One of your most vocal state senators has published a report strongly suggesting that your faculty is dining high on the public trough but working very few hours for the privilege.

In your annual state-of-the-university address to the faculty, you must announce further cutbacks and more layoffs.

You are scheduled to meet with your institution's most influential alumni group. You know they dearly loved your predecessor, whose priorities were athletics and old-school traditions. You must tell them that times have changed.

A donor capable of making a multimillion-dollar gift to your institution has been primed and cultivated. Now you are in his palatial home on a mission: to ask for more money than seems decent.

Once upon a time, there really was an ivory tower. Life was different behind the campus walls. Day stretched into peaceful day, with only a few harmless student pranks to ruffle the waters of academic discourse. And the world beyond seemed content to leave well enough alone. Visits from the press were rare occasions. A few well-heeled alumni could be counted on for largesse from time to time.

That world has gone the way of professors in black gowns in the classroom and white-glove teas on Sundays in the women's dormitory.

Now what goes on at colleges and universities is very interesting to the world beyond. Local communities make town-gown relations lively and sometimes contentious. State legislators and their constituents are firmly convinced that colleges and universities waste taxpayers' money just for spite. Student athletes draw national attention from sports writers. Tragedies such as drug-related deaths or rapes on campus are features on the evening news and the national talk shows.

And you are the primary spokesperson, the last word, and the first among the fall guys for your institution. There's no way to hide, delegate, or breeze through this responsibility. As leader, it falls to you to speak for the university or college. It's very important to do that well.

THE GROUND RULES

Forget your mother's advice about avoiding the spotlight. You weren't hired to stay in the background, modest and demure. On many occasions, you are the institution for the public in general and for the media and prospective donors in particular. Your every word will be measured, your appearance scrutinized, and your attitude judged.

It's best, then, to cover as many bases as you can before the television lights glare or the black-tie dinner begins. You already have a head start if you have developed your personal and interpersonal skills.

Appearance

Most of us don't have the features and figure of a super-model. (If you do, ignore this section and revel in your great good fortune.) Still, it's possible to put one's best face forward in matters of grooming and dress. Conservative is your watchword here. The goal is to be neutral but not dull. Neat haircuts and no shaving nicks on men and subtle makeup and "business" hairdos for women are essential. Adopt a very limited color palette in clothing for both sexes: black, gray, navy, brown, tan for suits and jackets— white and pastel colors for shirts. Of course, your shoes will be polished and free of signs of wear. If you use a cologne (and it's better not to), make sure it is very lightly applied. Your nails should be short and well manicured. Your jewelry should be real gold or silver and always understated.

Etiquette

Good manners aren't difficult to acquire if you go by the principle that etiquette is simply a formalized attempt to put others at their ease. Seating guests, opening doors, standing when greeting, and even knowing the right fork to use are all ways to ensure that social occasions run smoothly with the least chance of giving offense. If you were not well schooled in etiquette as a younger person, it behooves you to read widely on the subject or take a course so that doing the right thing is second nature to you.

Mixing and Mingling

Understand that, as a leader, you are a bigger deal than when you are a follower. People really are honored to meet you. Sometimes this will happen only once for them, so make the occasion memorable. As you move through a room filled with constituents, exude warmth. Smile, shake hands, make eye contact, and use names whenever possible.

Standing on Ceremony

While you will be observed closely under more casual circumstances, you will be under the microscope at formal or ceremonial events. Whether you are attending a kindergarten graduation or presiding over commencement for 20,000 students, you need to treat each event as if it had world-changing consequences. Sometimes that's true. You need to wear your robes—and even your funny hat—with dignity and pride. As you recognize individuals with citations and awards, show your genuine appreciation. And stay awake! Even though this may be your 40th convocation, it's the first for almost everyone else.

SPEAKING OUT LOUD

Public speaking occasions are fewer in number in this electronic age. There are many other, more efficient ways to get the word out. Nevertheless, there will be many times in a leader's career when stepping boldly up to the podium to make a formal speech is necessary.

Most people admit to at least some mild fear of public speaking. For others the word *terror* is more appropriate. Even the most seasoned speaker worries about his or her performance. It's an awesome thing to face a group of people with nothing between you and them but a flimsy stand. There are some guidelines that can help.

First, *make sure the message is simple.* The listener should come away with one or possibly two ideas, not a whole monograph with an annotated bibliography. Follow the tried and true formula of (1) telling them what you're going to tell them, (2) telling them, and (3) telling them what you told them. Of course you'll be more subtle than that, and you'll take pains to write the speech so that it is entertaining, thought provoking, and clear. But the formula works.

Second, *use illustrations.* Back up each statement with down-to-earth examples, anecdotes, statistics, and stories. Compelling speeches are rich in detail and allow listeners to make connections between your words and their lives.

Third, *be wary of any audiovisual aids* that you are not completely comfortable using. A picture may be worth a thousand words, but not when it's stuck in the slide carousel or out of sequence in the PowerPoint presentation. Handouts are another matter. They can be very helpful, especially as illustrations for very complex information. Time their distribution to the audience, though. It's human nature to read what's put in front of you, and you want people to be listening to you.

Finally, make it a point to *develop your skill as a speaker* so that your delivery is strong and smooth. Observe speakers you admire. Talk your family and friends into letting you practice in front of them. Decide what method you will use to keep on track—a full text of the speech, note cards, teleprompter—and practice with it many times.

No one expects you to become a star. In fact, appearing to be too slick can be a problem in some organizations. However, it is possible to achieve a polished performance.

MEETING THE PRESS

Too many leaders, in my view, see the press as a necessary evil if not a downright adversary. It's true that many a leader has been stung by rough treatment at the hands of reporters. And virtually every leader has been misquoted or has had words taken out of context.

But never forget that the press is your link to a mass audience. There is simply no other way to reach as many people simultaneously with your message. While reporters can and do report your organization's problems, crises, and scandals, they will also print your good news. And they will do so without charging you a dime.

Leaders are well advised, then, to learn about the media and how best to deal with them. Here are some points to consider:

- Tell the truth. Reporters will find out anyway and might make things much worse for you. Admit to mistakes and be up front about the ways in which you will be addressing problems.
- Respond quickly. While you don't need to react without a plan, you do need to get back to reporters as soon as you can—within a few hours of their call always, if only to say that you can't make a statement yet.
- Understand the reporters' perspective. They know that they must entertain their readers and viewers or else their work will be ignored (and advertisers will desert them). Unfortunately, most people are entertained by bad news rather than good. Therefore, be prepared to see your positive financial news or new projects receive less space than the latest string of burglaries in the residence halls.
- If you don't wish to be quoted on a particularly sensitive topic, keep quiet. Going "off the record" is dangerous, no matter how trustworthy the reporter appears to be. Remember, he or she is searching for news, and your offhand remarks about possible layoffs, for example, would make a great headline.
- If you sense antagonism in the reporter, or if the questions become badgering, keep your cool. It helps to remember that this is not an attack on you personally. But in any case, your intemperate display of anger will certainly make it to the evening news while your thoughtful responses may never see the light of day.
- If you don't know the answer to a reporter's question, say so. But always offer to provide the information later and then make good on your promise.
- Keep your responses short and offer examples to illustrate your points.
- Don't let reporters put words in your mouth. Listen very carefully to their questions. Some can be like the age-old, no-win query, "Have you stopped beating your dog?"
- Accept that you won't always get good press and that, yes, you will be misquoted once in a while. That may simply be a function of a fast-paced world, not a media vendetta against you and your organization.

FUND-RAISING

No matter how large or professional your fund-raising staff, you will put in some, perhaps many, hours preparing to ask—and then asking for—money for your organization. For large organizations, the ask may be in the millions of dollars, but even for modest amounts, the assistance, support, and often physical presence of the leader can mean the difference between rejection and success.

Good fund-raising begins with your deep commitment to the organization. It rests on your vision for its future and your intimate knowledge of its mission as a unique institution. Only then can you help donors understand how important their support is and how they can be part of the organization's progress.

You can expect your development people to provide you with a great deal of information, printed materials, and advice and counsel. They will do most of the preliminary work, including many hours of face-to-face contact with a potential donor.

You can also assume that your participation in an ask will be limited to only major gifts from donors who have been cultivated over the years. As leader, you have a special kind of clout, but it must be used sparingly and judiciously.

Development staff people have expectations of their leaders, too. First, they want you to *be committed to advancement.* You will need to devote time and energy to raising funds as well as provide inspiration and vision.

They want you to *maintain your credibility* by being consistent in your communications with donors. In other words, refrain from the temptation to accept funds for projects and programs that don't fit your vision and could steer the institution in another direction.

You will be asked to *be both persistent and patient.* Major gifts almost always arrive after years of cultivation. It is frustrating to devote precious time to a potential donor who refuses one request after another or who is unreasonably demanding. However, staying the course regardless of the obstacles could yield badly needed funds for your organization.

You will be expected *to remain optimistic.* Fund-raising is often an exhausting process that leads to nothing in the end. Great expectations are shot down as often as they are met. But you must always support the idea that success is possible and just around the corner.

CHAPTER 7

Hard Experience

Experience is a good teacher, but her fees are very high.
—W. R. Inge

O nce upon a time there was a university president who had learned all the lessons of higher education leadership. He knew how to conduct well-timed meetings, say just enough in his speeches, and write pithy, memorable messages. He knew enough about budget matters to make wise decisions while leaving the day-to-day work to his senior staff. He relied on a personal staff for up-to-the-minute information, so he was never caught unaware.

He was a sought-after coach for junior staff and faculty, he was savvy in the ways of government, and he had an acute sense of timing in matters requiring empathy and caring. He had mastered the art of remembering dozens of names and displayed an uncanny sense about personnel. Best of all, he had a finely honed perspective on life that led him quickly to what was really important. Too bad he's now 98 and retired.

If only we could make use of all the experience we acquire over the course of our higher education careers! Unfortunately, like our fairy-tale president, when we've gathered up the wisdom of the years, we'll be in our dotage. Still, it's possible to borrow some lessons from those who've come before us.

In this chapter I offer you some insights I wish I had had a few years ago. These are the kinds of things graduate school advisors and first-job mentors sometimes forget in their zeal to help shape you into a teacher and scholar.

And they are the things I've learned through hard experience. Perhaps if you can take some of these to heart, your path will be softer and easier.

That said, read and apply where relevant.

MANAGING TO SUCCEED

The 35 Percent Rule

Most activities last 35 percent longer than they should. That may be a cynical view, but think about some common examples. Take a televised football game—it requires at least a three-and-a-half to four-hour commitment, and that's just for the viewer at home. The die-hard season ticket holder fights traffic both ways to get to and from his or her seat and often devotes seven hours to this purpose. Wouldn't a 35 percent cut in time be a boon?

Then there are baseball games—lessons in endurance for many. Just how many times does the pitcher really have to wipe his brow? And what about sermons? It's a rare Sunday when parishioners leave saying, "What a great sermon! I just wish it had been longer." Must weddings stretch into hours of ceremony and revelry? And why must retirement dinners allow speaker after speaker podium time to say things like, "I was asked to talk for three minutes, but I simply can't do justice to dear old Charlie in such a short time." No wonder attendees cringe between bites of chocolate mousse.

If brevity is the soul of wit, then there are some really dull events going on. But, you say, there's nothing I can do about these activities. I'm just one person, after all. True, but as one person—particularly one person in charge of a higher education institution—you will find many ways to apply the 35 percent rule and win many admirers in the process.

Speeches

Sometimes the trouble with having a fine mind and the wisdom of experience is the corresponding urge to share with all and sundry. We work hard to make every point and support each point with numerous examples and appropriate citations from other experts in the field. And all too often, eyes glaze over about half-way through our presentations.

Try to apply the 35 percent rule this way. Write the speech as you normally would, points and supporting evidence included. Then ask yourself what the main points are. There really should be only very few, often just one. A new student convocation speech, for example, might be summarized as, "You'll need to commit at least 40 hours a week to studying outside the classroom to succeed here at Olde Ivy," or as, "Diversity of programs, services, and people are what make State U. a distinct institution." An annual address might be captured as, "The financial picture is very promising. Now let us press forward to ensure that teaching matters most here at the University of Perpetual Responsibility."

Look at the speech again. Where there are sub-points, examples, and citations that have nothing directly to do with your main points, cut. Be unmerciful. And if you can't bring yourself to deep-six some of your profound prose, then ask a good writer to do it for you.

Remember that it's the audience that matters here, not you. Better to leave them saying, "He's a hero to all, women and men: They gave him 15 minutes and he finished in 10."

Staff Meetings

There's much more information on conducting productive meetings in chapter 4. If you follow the principles offered there, you should have meetings that run about 35 percent shorter than commonly expected. Of course, this takes a great deal of practice, but as a leader in higher education you'll never run out of meetings from which to learn.

Trustee Meetings

It's true that trustees, your employers, set the agenda for their meetings, and the chair is in charge. That is as it should be. Nevertheless, you can offer suggestions to streamline the process. Why, for example, are staff reports, which are usually mailed out ahead of time, read cover to cover at these meetings? A summary would suffice in the majority of cases, possibly shaving the time by the magic 35 percent. But even if you can manage just a 20 percent trimming, you'll emerge as a hero for some very important people.

Ceremonies

Convocations and commencements tend to come at the hottest and stickiest times of the year. These are also times of high anxiety—new students wondering whether they'll have a good time in college; or high fatigue—students on the way out having mastered the art of having a very good time until all hours of the morning. And at both of these occasions are the parents, family members, and friends who have a strong need to get in and out as quickly as seems polite.

These factors taken together point to well-planned, appropriately pompous, and blessedly brief ceremonies. One way to accomplish this is to eliminate all unnecessary speakers. If possible, stick to one student representative, one university official (usually you), and, if required, one outside celebrity. Limit each of these speakers to 12 minutes or less.

If previous ceremonies at your institution traditionally included speeches by every key officer and dean, you will be injuring some egos when you adopt the lean and meaningful approach. But the true honorees—the students and their families—will be forever in your debt.

I know it can be done. At one mid-sized university, commencement for more than 3,000 students now lasts about an hour and a half, marching in and marching out included.

As applied in this chapter, the rule pared my original number of suggestions by at least 35 percent. It works.

Managing Time

I know you've been advised that you can't do everything you'd like and that you must learn to manage your time. But I'll bet that you don't quite believe that if you are just starting out in higher education leadership, full of youthful enthusiasm.

I will tell you that you must embrace these concepts or face some heavy consequences. What you decide to do and not to do will, in large measure, determine your success. Some suggestions follow.

Link Your Time with Your Vision

Know which of your activities are the most likely to help your institution reach its vision. Will it be curriculum reform? Placing a greater emphasis on teaching? Attracting a diverse faculty? Hiring some star scholars? Increasing the endowment?

Pick the two or three most important ones and spend the majority of your time there. Apply the 35 percent rule to cut down on other activities to make this possible.

Slow Down

Make certain that the usual frenetic pace of higher education doesn't consume you. Yes, you will put in an extraordinary number of hours on the job, and, yes, it will seem as though your time is never your own. But you can and must plan for some uninterrupted time to preserve your sanity.

One colleague gets to the office an hour and a half before anyone else. He uses that time for letter writing, planning, and just plain thinking about the day, the week, and the month ahead. So when his wife asks the night before what his day is going to be like, he can honestly say, "I'm not entirely sure, but when it gets here, I'll be ready." Another colleague does the same sort of thing in the early evening hours when he can, though the great number of evening obligations that come with the office make this practice somewhat risky.

Sundays are the days many leaders reserve for quiet time with their families. One colleague regularly blocks out 90 minutes of the day for this purpose—not easy, but it can be done.

The commonality of these reserved periods is the prohibition of phone calls or other interruptions, unless there is an emergency. And even if something important comes up, I've learned that most things can wait for an hour or so. Whatever the technique, each of us must find a way to balance work and relaxation.

Select Your Meetings

Ask yourself whether your presence is really required at a particular meeting or event. On rare occasions, you can skip some of these. Keep in mind that your attendance lends an air of authority to the occasion and signals to the rest of the community that the meeting or reception is important. Attending too few will prompt some to criticize you for being an isolationist. Attending too many dilutes the impact of your office.

When you decide that you really must be there, know ahead of time what goals must be accomplished and what your role will be. Have your staff do the legwork for you and provide you with information in whatever form suits you best. If you retain best during a face-to-face pre-event meeting, insist on that. If having information written in a particular way (summary, outline, bullets) helps, make certain that that is how it is provided.

For further guidance, see chapter 4 for suggestions on running a productive meeting.

The Budget

When it comes to the intricacies of the budget, accept that you can't know everything. You will need to know more about the overall budget than your key staff members, except for your chief budget officer. Your staff will have detailed knowledge about their own particular areas (and they will press you hard for more funds in those areas). Your role is to ensure that the institution's funding follows its mission and vision.

Keep It Simple

Insist that budget matters are explained to you and to others. In spite of complexities, they can be put in lay terms. Let it be known that confusion is the presenter's problem, not the audience's. Budget matters are not hard to understand when kept at a conceptual level.

Insist on Honesty

It might be possible to be fooled once, but if it happens a second time it means someone has made a serious mistake. Make it clear to your staff that you expect to be kept informed and to be given accurate information, no matter how bad the news might be.

Be Conservative

You can be certain that there will be a healthy tension between your budget officer and the rest of your staff. She or he will be the most conservative member of the team, holding the key to the strongbox for all she or he is worth. Your job is to ensure that your staff work out their differences.

When I was a vice president for academic affairs, I learned quickly that the best way to achieve my goals was to work with the vice president for business and finance first. That way, we could go to the president as a united front, which would make our lives (and the president's) easier. You can help your staff adopt this method.

You must also hold the long view of the institution so you and your staff can make wise decisions. It turns out that being conservative in budget matters is most often the wisest choice. A faculty member at one institution pressed his president for a significantly greater portion of the endowment for his department. He reasoned that the 20 percent rate of growth would continue and that a payout of similar magnitude made sense. His president chose to offer context by refusing this request. Criticized by the faculty member for being too conservative, he responded that no president he'd ever known about had ever been fired for erring on the side of caution, but there were several whose desire for rapid progress had stripped away precious resources.

The Need to Know

In a large and complex higher education environment where information seems to create itself daily, it is impossible to know about everything that's going on. Nevertheless, it's critical that you avoid, at all costs, walking into situations unprepared—like finding out you're the emcee of an event when you walk in the door; that a rape case was a false alarm; that only a portion of the funding from the state is really coming through.

Considering that one human being—especially one who's juggling many priorities at once—can absorb only so much information, there has to be a support system in place. That's why you must have staff members whose job is to prepare you in advance. Cultivate people who are quick to assess a situation, who know the right people to call, who can tap resources like the library and the Internet, and who can summarize efficiently.

How prepared do you need to be? My rule of thumb is to be more knowledgeable about any given subject than anyone else in the room, except the experts. If you find yourself knowing more than the experts, you are either spending too much time on the details or you have weak experts. Both situations need to be corrected. You'll be most effective when you have a broad knowledge about the important things, a detailed knowledge of selected things, and a staff of people who are extremely well versed in their particular areas.

Win the Game, Not Necessarily the Point

The game is advancing your institution. You do that by accumulating "points" toward the advancement of your institution slowly but surely. But you don't have to win every point to win. In fact, sometimes it's good to lose one or two. Here's an example. In one state it was standard operating procedure for members of the Senate Budget Committee to beat up on the presidents of their higher education system every year at budget hearings. And the presidents were expected to absorb the criticism while defending the institution politely and passively.

Naturally they didn't look forward to this annual event. While nearly all the legislators took their shots, one senator in particular gave them a very hard time. This person took pains to be offensive and degrading to the president and the system. One of the presidents, banking on the fact that this senator did not have a great deal of respect, elected to retaliate one year. As the senator made incorrect or unsubstantiated claims, the president corrected this misinformation authoritatively and, unfortunately, condescendingly. He emerged as a hero to his colleagues in higher education and he won a number of points. But he lost the game. His system's budget was reduced by the amount of his personal salary by the full senate. In solidarity, the other senators drew ranks around their publicly humiliated colleague.

Winning the point can be very satisfying. Winning the game is much more so.

Beware the One-Trick Pony

Impressive though he may be, the one-trick pony can count with one hoof—but that's all. His counterpart in the organization is the firebrand, high-energy, charming person who has only one skill and no aptitude to pick up others.

This is the candidate who can soon have a search committee eating out of his hands. When a colleague asked just one implementation question (see page 65) of such a candidate, he got a detailed and thorough analysis of the problem presented plus a long list of solutions. While some of the solutions were clearly unworkable, this committee ascribed this fact to a creative mind and virtually hired the candidate on the spot.

Once onboard, it became embarrassingly clear that this person had just this one trick up his sleeve. Just this one. And even this plan soon showed its frayed edges, since it called for resources beyond the institution's capabilities. But Mr. One-Trick couldn't grasp the concept of trade-offs, no matter how many times it was explained.

He was, to paraphrase Clark Kerr, the person who came in fired with enthusiasm and who left the same way.

Painstaking research about a candidate's previous experience, plus a thoughtful interview process that includes a number of problem analysis/solution questions, quickly unmasks one-trick ponies.

One Day a Peacock—The Next a Feather Duster

This was a phrase that one of my friends loved to use. I laughed when I heard it the first time and at each subsequent telling, because I liked this person very much. But though the phrase lost its originality, the truth it embodies remains.

As in the fame/shame syndrome examples in appendix B, leaders in this field find ample opportunities to shine and to flounder. And it's important to accept both with equanimity. Believing that your peacock status will last indefinitely will bring you right up to the brick wall of disappointment. But worrying that your feather duster feeling will last can cloud your view to the next opportunity to get up there with those eagles again. Am I tripping over my avian metaphors?

Keep in mind that good times and bad times share one immutable characteristic: they always pass.

PLEASING PEOPLE

The Difficult Person Index

Like good art, difficult people are hard to describe but easy to recognize. We now openly talk about difficult people; there's even a diagnostic classification for them. Contrary to popular opinion, there are not more of these in higher education, but on some days that's hard to believe. Nevertheless, if the leader isn't careful, the difficult person will absorb his or her every waking moment.

I believe that most difficult people are not malicious. In fact, many champion causes well worth our support. It's just that their single-mindedness and inflexibility are hard to take for long periods of time. Unfortunately they usually go on for long periods of time because they seem unable to pick up the social cues that signal to the rest of us that it's time to stop talking.

The chair of a colleague's board of trustees was a difficult person. He classified people into three categories: fools, liars, and incompetents. University officials referred tongue-in-cheek to those he accused of being all three as "winning the trifecta." There were several winners. My colleague sent several of his staff to a two-day conference to learn how to deal with this difficult chairperson. They came back with some great ideas, though the difficult person remained resolutely difficult.

I asked another colleague if she could name some characteristics of a typical difficult person. Here's what she said: "They won't go through channels. In fact, they are quite happy to call you at home at all sorts of inconvenient times. They'll take on the slightest matter as a personal crusade. Dirty restrooms, the quality of blackboard chalk, the true meaning of the institution's motto—they're all the same to the difficult person. Even when they do follow channels, they tell a slightly different story to each listener, making it very difficult to determine what the exact problem is. The sound of their own voice is music to their ears and they play on and on. The usual ratio is one hour of talk to five minutes of substance. And to top it all off, after one hour of your precious time they'll inform you that they've already talked to their local legislator about this problem since they knew you'd be no help."

It is useless to resist the difficult person. The struggle will only exhaust you. Acknowledging this helps. There are other strategies.

Avoid Institutions with a High Difficult Person Index

You can learn this by asking strategic questions during the long process of courtship between you and the institution. For comparison, assume that the normal index is about 1 percent. Thus a 2 percent index is a recipe for big trouble. At a university with about 2,000 faculty and staff plus some 10,000 students, a 2 percent index leads to 240 individuals whose complaints and schemes will significantly erode time that would certainly be better spent elsewhere. And that will be true no matter how masterfully you delegate and how jealously you guard your schedule.

So if you discover that an institution is known for harboring more than its fair share of difficult people, say thank you to any offer you might receive and move on.

Accept Some Intrusions

You will need to give difficult people some of your time, of course. Allow for a 20-minute appointment but orchestrate ahead of time an interruption by your secretary who will have pressing business for you to attend to. This works best about 15 minutes into your meeting since it gives the person some summing up time.

If you have the luxury, appoint a "special assistant in charge of difficult people." This must be someone who is the soul of patience and empathy and whose listening skills rival those of the Sphinx. He or she must have enough prestige to impress others but not enough authority to make big decisions without your approval. Thus, the special assistant must consult with you before any action is taken. This won't happen often since it is the listening that really matters.

Failing a special assistant of this variety, you must make it clear to your key staff that they will be required to give a certain amount of their time to the difficult people on campus. In this way, the burden is dispersed rather than falling on your shoulders alone.

Never forget, though, that you have no real chance to make the difficult people on your watch happy. But they can certainly make you miserable if you let them.

Coaching

If you want to ensure the continuing success of your institution, be certain to devote time to coaching and mentoring those who will lead it in the future. While you won't be able to devote a great deal of your time to this work, it is an important part of any leadership position. Of course, your example is the best tool for mentorship. The respect you have earned will encourage younger leaders to model your approaches and adapt them for their own work.

There are other techniques, as well.

- Take the time to explain. Place issues in context. For example, your budget officer may well express frustration about the slow pace with which faculty, deans, and provosts make decisions. Help her or him understand that academic officers have a number of constituencies to consider and serve. They are also frequently dealing with highly complex matters. The budget officer may see clearly that consolidating similar courses would save money. The faculty, however, are aware of the shades of differences among the courses and the students' needs they serve.

  Faculty, too, may have difficulty with the conservative nature of institutional finance. Their passion for their discipline can cloud their appreciation for the institution's long-term fiscal health.

  And many of your staff may chafe at student discipline problems. "Why," they ask, "can't the student affairs officer just clamp down on these kids?" They might appreciate one colleague's take on student expectations of the dean of student affairs as "part concierge, part bodyguard, and part social worker."

- Share information. Copy articles to send to your staff, suggest further reading, encourage attendance at conferences, and foster links with their counterparts at other institutions through professional organizations and the like. Make certain that at least part of their time is spent furthering their own growth.

  Mentoring can well be one of the most satisfying parts of your leadership. It is a privilege to watch the people with whom you work develop their strengths, knowing that you've had a part in this process.

Working with the Government

Finding ways to work cooperatively with state government is a given if you're leading one of the nation's many fine state institutions. But even if you work exclusively for private colleges and universities, managing an effective government relations program is essential. Here are some things to remember.

- Cultivate legislators' staff members. As important as the senators, councilmembers, and governors are, their staffs deserve special attention. These are the men and women who can be very helpful (or very unhelpful) to you and your cause. Make sure you and your key staff get to know them well and show appreciation when they've made efforts on your behalf, whether or not your goals were reached.

- Don't cry wolf. Paint an accurate picture of the consequences of budget cutbacks in higher education. If the results will seriously affect your ability to educate the state's students, it will become very clear without your claiming that the sky is falling. I heard the story of a chancellor who claimed that a state cutback would make it necessary to increase tuition by 10 percent and that action would greatly decrease enrollments. The cut was made and the tuition raised, but enrollment stayed the same, damaging the chancellor's credibility for some time to come.

- Respond to requests. Legislators and other government officials will come to you asking for special treatment for constituents seeking admission to your institution or jobs on your campus. Make certain that your staff gives these requests all due attention. A prospective student, for example, should meet with one of your admissions counselors. If he or she is academically marginal, options like summer school should be explored.

Don't lower your standards or break the rules to meet one of these requests. Simply make sure that every "t" is crossed and "i" is dotted in these cases. And let the requestor know that you have followed through on his or her constituents' behalf.

Friends

Have a group of trusted friends, but count them on one hand. Good friends are there for you when you need them. They are people with whom you can relax and let go of the burdens of your office. Unfortunately, being a higher education leader does not lend itself to a large circle of friends. You will meet many people whom you like and who like you. But your very busy schedule will make it difficult to form close, sustained relationships.

It's also true that a wide circle of friends can sap your charismatic power (see chapter 3) quickly. First of all, a president with many friends probably has a fair share of hangers-on with their own agendas. Second, being everyone's friend means that you're like everyone else. And to be an effective leader, you need to be a little bit different from the mainstream.

Herein lies one of the paradoxes of leadership. As human beings, leaders have the same need as others for the intimacy that comes with close relationships. However, the jobs we take on preclude forming a number of such relationships. That is why those of us with spouses or significant others with whom intimacies can be shared are blessed.

Do seek out three or four friendships from among your board, perhaps, or from the wider community. And keep close ties with a few colleagues from institutions you have served. But don't expect to enjoy the same kinds of friendships that many others have. You must establish the distance that enables you to lead effectively.

The Name Game

While I know it can be perilous to admit personal failings to a wide audience, I confess here that I have a terrible time remembering names. Faces, hometowns, even personal quirks stay imbedded in my mind way past their usefulness, but names seem to skip off my cerebral cortex and into the ozone.

And if not remembering a person's name is bad practice, it's worse to call them by the wrong name. I've done that, too, I'm afraid. Once I gave an effusive speech thanking a donor for his largesse and consistently referred to him by the wrong name. To compound my error, I called him by the name of his rival in business.

Matters aren't improved when someone adopts a "difficult person" tactic of shaking my hand and looking deep into my eyes saying, "You don't remember me, do you?" I'm either proved a liar by saying I do know the name or proved memory-impaired by confessing that I don't.

I know people like to be called by name on a second or subsequent meeting. When someone remembers our name we feel important and valued. And I've tried hard to overcome this problem.

I've heard that it helps to repeat a person's name when you shake his or her hand while at the same time associating one of his or her characteristics with his or her name. Ms. Lee, for example, may strike you as a very happy person, so you think, "Glee = Lee." The story goes that a president was delighted to have this new method at his disposal when he was introduced to a new donor. The donor's name was Smith and he had a full beard. The association was Smith = Smith Brothers' Cough Drops. When my colleague met this man a second time, he shook his hand firmly and said, brimming with confidence, "How nice to see you, Mr. Ludens."

If you have no trouble remembering names, you are very fortunate. But if you are like most higher education leaders who meet hundreds of people monthly, you may struggle in this area. It helps to have staff members brief you ahead of time. Ask them to help you remember the names of just a few of the key people you will meet. If appropriate, encourage the use of name tags with big print, though asking your board members to wear them is stretching it. If your spouse or companion is good at names, keep him or her by your side as often as you can.

When all else fails, and it will, accept the name problem and become a practiced apologizer. Most people will understand. Those who don't probably wouldn't be happy under any circumstances.

Random Acts of Kindness

Here I'm referring to the small gestures that will be long remembered: the birthday cards, the sympathy letters, the visits to the hospital, the one-on-one time for those in distress. Your schedule won't permit your doing as many of these as you might like, but they are still important. First, expressing your appreciation and concern will make you feel better. Reaching out to others expresses our own personal values in a fulfilling way.

Your example will help others in your organization to do the same and thereby establish a culture where kindness is practiced and expected. And your good works will solidify the perception of you as a leader who cares.

These gestures need not be excessive or ostentatious and certainly they need to be appropriate to the need. Don't rely exclusively on your own instincts. Ask staff members—perhaps that special assistant in charge of difficult people—to remind you or send a note or card on your behalf.

Trade-Offs

On a rational level, we grasp the concept that it's not possible to please all the people all the time. But emotionally, most of us cling to the notion that we can have and can do what we want if we try hard enough or if others are cooperative enough.

Americans, for instance, want a balanced budget while at the same time they want all their entitlements fulfilled. They don't want to know about the downside or the unintended consequences of particular actions. It's no surprise, then, to see this same attitude prevalent on university campuses.

SAMPLE BUDGET SUMMARY SHEET
To be used as the basis of a trade-offs exercise

($Millions)

	Year 1	Year 2	Year 3	Year 4	Year 5
Potential Negatives					
1. Salary budget increments; added cost if each year is 1% higher	($1.8)	($3.6)	($5.5)	($7.6)	($9.8)
2. Increment general operating budgets by 2% per year	($0.6)	($1.2)	($1.8)	($2.5)	($3.2)
3. Tuition increase of 4.5% instead of 5% per year	($0.8)	($1.6)	($2.4)	($3.4)	($4.4)
4. Room and board increases of 3.5% instead of 4% per year	($0.3)	($0.5)	($0.8)	($1.1)	($1.4)
5. Continuing education enrollment decline of 2% per year instead of projected 1% per year	($0.2)	($0.5)	($0.8)	($1.1)	($1.4)
Potential Positives					
1. Tuition discount rate declines from 37% to 36%	$2.0	$2.1	$2.2	$2.3	$2.4
2. Attrition declines from 9% to 8%	$0.6	$1.3	$2.0	$2.8	$3.1
3. Additional 100 FTE tuition-paying graduate students	$0.4	$1.2	$1.6	$1.6	$1.6
4. Employee health insurance cost increase 6% instead of 7%	$0.2	$0.3	$0.5	$0.7	$0.9

Faculty push for salary increases, students protest tuition hikes, and staff petition for more benefits. And no one addresses the availability of resources to meet all these demands.

One president told me that faculty morale on his campus was nearly always scraping bottom. "I have a hard time being sympathetic," he said, "since they are one of the highest paid faculties in our region. Yet," he told me, "they complained about the less-than-exceptional computer infrastructure and about insufficient operating budgets to meet instructional priorities. What they don't seem to grasp or want to acknowledge is the inverse relationship between their salaries and funding other institutional needs."

I sympathize, but I also see this as an opportunity to exercise good leadership by explaining the need for trade-offs. The more the decision-making process is placed in the context of the whole organization's priorities, the more people tend to buy into the choices that are made.

One institution developed a summary page outlining the costs of various initiatives (see Sample Budget Summary Sheet, page 89). It formed the basis of the president's discussion sessions at each of the university's schools and colleges, at staff forums, and at student meetings. At each, the president challenged people to select their top three priorities. If, for example, the majority supported increasing salaries by 1 percent more than the projected amount, and it translated to an additional annual outlay of $1.5 million, the president asked where those funds should be drawn. Would raising tuition be the answer? Cutbacks in the operating budget? A reduction in benefits? The discussions that followed helped attendees begin to comprehend the tension between aspirations and resources. And slowly the notion of trade-offs began to take hold.

This is not to say that wishful thinking was banished. People still didn't want to acknowledge that meeting one need diminished resources for another. But they were able to understand more clearly the realities of budgeting.

Good News/Bad News

Would that life was a series of good news, one happy circumstance after another. Of course, it's not. The story you tell about your institution will include hard-to-accept facts like job layoffs, embarrassing moments like fraternity brawls, and unwelcome news like the end of a program.

That's why you need to have a solid communications strategy on which to rely. As I mentioned in chapter 6, honesty and forthrightness with the press is essential if for no other reason than the inevitability of the truth emerging. This is just as true when you are dealing with your internal constituencies. Borrowing from students of Machiavelli, I suggest that you disseminate bad news—all of it—right away. Let the good news dribble out bit by bit.

On one campus, budget difficulties of significant proportions loomed on the horizon. But instead of laying out the whole story, the leader there chose to report the need for cuts in May, salary freezes in December, and layoffs the following April. By that time, the campus community was in turmoil. Members' trust had been violated, and, instead of coming together to deal with problems, a bunker mentality prevailed in which each unit hoarded limited resources and waited for the next round of bad news to hit.

Good news, however, should be relished right down to the last bit. A plan to increase salaries should be announced when it's certain that this happy event will take place. The group working on this plan should report their progress regularly. This news is also an occasion to reinforce the message that things are looking up. And the implementation of the plan should receive broad coverage with all the appropriate fanfare.

CHAPTER 8

Conclusion

Here's the material in the previous chapters in an easy-to-skim format. The do's and don'ts are useful as reminders, especially when your tether is getting shorter and you are wondering why you started this leadership thing in the first place. As you review my suggestions, think about what you might have done differently and imagine the story you will tell five to 10 years from now. Then read the section in this chapter on the selection and training of future academic leaders for some insight into new ideas on the horizon.

DO'S AND DON'TS

- Do be ready and willing to restate your vision often. But don't be afraid to credit others; it helps make it their vision too.
- Do be introspective enough to know your strengths and weaknesses and to recognize your successes and failures. You can learn from both.
- Find colleagues whose strengths balance your weaknesses and who will fortify your strengths. Make sure these are people who, like you, are willing to forgo personal needs for the greater good.
- Do develop a healthy respect for the use of power in achieving your goals. Remember that the legitimate power that comes with your

position is yours to lose by failing to act like a leader. Expert power resides within you but only in limited ways. Charismatic power can be cultivated without a complete makeover, particularly if you exercise the other forms of power judiciously.

- Do learn to lead a group by committing yourself to acquiring the necessary skills. Then create an environment that enables everyone to work effectively in groups as participants and as leaders. That could well be your most important legacy.

- Do be inclusive when you form committees and other groups. However, don't lose sight of the principle of least group size. Have too many people and you can't expect great results, except perhaps a fine social gathering.

- Do be a change agent—not for change's sake but for the sake of your institution, which will grow stronger as it evolves. Be prepared to support change publicly and often, but be just as prepared to back up your words with action.

- Know your institution's culture and respect it. But don't be so reverent that you begin to believe that change would be sacrilegious (even though some will try hard to convince you that would be so).

- Don't dwell on institutional failures, but be ready to admit that an initiative just plain didn't reach its potential. You will be respected for your honesty and forgiven for your mistakes (provided that it doesn't happen more than a few times).

- Do celebrate diversity, but don't apologize for the lack of perfection. Progress is not synonymous with constant harmony; progress comes from acknowledging differences, which can often be a messy process.

- Do expect civility. Of course you practice it yourself, but don't fall apart in the face of rudeness and disrespect. Instead, remember that you are the first among equals and you are being closely observed, especially when conflict arises.

- Do believe that talented and dedicated associates can be trusted to make things happen. This isn't an excuse to sit back, relax, and let the chips fall where they may. You must provide direction when necessary. Remember, though, that your primary role is as the keeper of the vision.

- Do expect loyalty from your colleagues—loyalty to you, to the institution, and, most important, to the vision.

- Don't assume that those who disagree with you are your enemies. When a colleague expresses a view different from yours, step back for a moment to assess how her or his perspective meshes with the institutional vision. Even if you still disagree, you aren't necessarily antagonists.
- Don't accept constant anxiety and tension as part of your job. Leading should also be fun and rewarding. And you can't be effective if you're always exhausted and stressed. If you are, either change your perspective or change jobs.
- Don't confide in everyone. You can be sure that your foibles will be discussed at length over the water cooler, but you don't need to feed the rumor mill with your true confessions. Have one or two very close and absolutely trustworthy friends so you can share confidences when you must, but keep that circle tight.
- Don't try to change the world. Leaders need to know what can be done, what simply can't be done, and what is possible with extra effort. Reaching beyond the expected is invigorating. Tilting at windmills isn't.
- Don't be dismayed if you lose your temper once in a great while. If losing control becomes a regular occurrence, though, take whatever steps are necessary to calm down.
- Don't be overly impressed with the fealty you get in the first few months and years of your leadership. You really aren't that charismatic and clever. Enjoy the attention while it's there, but don't put too much stock in your early reviews.
- Don't take criticism to heart. Expect to be blamed for things with which you had nothing to do. Your legacy will come from the long pull, not from the incident of the moment.
- Don't overanalyze your behavior and motives. Of course you'll devote some time and energy to your failures so you can learn from them. But dwelling on mistakes will only slow you down.
- Do understand that different people are motivated by different rewards. Find out what works and apply motivators as appropriate.
- Do love yourself. Be prepared, however, to change and to grow professionally and personally.
- Do have other interests. Your relationships with loved ones should be a high priority; so should entertainment, relaxation, and hobbies. Naturally you want to do well in your job, but don't let yourself be consumed by it.

- Do be proactive when defining the issues, but less so when suggesting solutions. And be the first to single out others for praise and recognition.
- Do use conflict constructively and help others to do the same. Take opportunities to reassure others that conflict is an acceptable and often useful fact of organizational life.
- Do know there are times when no compromise is possible, but be certain that your ego isn't getting in the way. Zero-sum games are rarely necessary.
- Do use the trappings of leadership. Just remember that they are part of the office, not your inalienable right. Once you step down, you'll be one of the many again.

Don't forget that the fun is in the trying. I never let myself think that all my efforts were successes. In fact, many of the "don'ts" you see in this book were things I tried or someone I observed tried and failed. I've learned from these errors and I try not to make them again. That doesn't mean I'm perfect; it just means that I make new mistakes.

To me, success comes from having realistic goals, doing what I can to reach them, evaluating where I am when I get there, and setting new goals. It's a cycle that, so far, hasn't stopped. I don't expect it to.

I hope you can make good use of the tools I've described in this book. I ask only one thing of you. Keep track of what you learn and add to the body of knowledge about this elusive thing called leadership.

THE SELECTION AND TRAINING OF FUTURE ACADEMIC LEADERS

This book has been about the skills I believe are necessary to lead. Some of you will consider my advice, ignore it, and carve your own path toward a top leadership position in higher education. Some of you will decide that this kind of leadership isn't for you. And some will go about acquiring and improving the skills I've defined. To me, any one of these three outcomes is acceptable as long as careful thought and consideration goes into the decision.

But beyond the personal level, what of the pool of future leaders? What can we do about enhancing that pool and helping new leaders make better decisions about their lives? Fortunately, seasoned professionals in higher education are working on this issue. My colleague Robert Diamond has been thinking long and hard about the need to improve the selection and training of future leaders. He has formed the National Academy for Academic Leadership, whose ultimate goal is improving the quality, effectiveness, and efficiency of teaching and learning at colleges and universities. This would be accomplished by helping present and future leaders develop the necessary skills and knowledge required to lead meaningful and systematic change in the academic enterprise. Right now the project is attracting funding, and Diamond expects the academy to be fully self-supported.

I believe that this project will make an important contribution to the continuous evolution of higher education. Certainly there are other such programs such as the highly regarded ACE Fellowship Program and the Harvard Leadership Program. But the Diamond proposal would serve a much larger number of people and at a number of critical levels on college campuses from department chairs on up.

Self-Selection

In chapter 5 I talked about how institutions can improve their chances of getting the right person for major positions. But even with the help of highly sophisticated search firms, assiduous reference checking, and carefully staged interviews, mistakes are often made. Usually this happens because the person and the institutional goals and culture clash. The best remedy here is to be sure that the match is a good one by asking more questions and by more carefully confronting possible disconnects.

Searches can also be unsuccessful because the committee cannot determine whether the individual has the necessary tools to be effective or because the individual is unaware of his or her own strengths and weaknesses (perhaps he or she didn't read my book!).

There is an approach that might prove particularly helpful to individuals who aspire to leadership. I caution that it can be effective only if the participants are assured that the information will be used solely for their personal development, not shared with others. Diamond's proposed academy and the ACE and Harvard programs, which maintain this kind of strict confidentiality, might well be places where the following approach could be tried.

Assessment Centers

Assessment centers, as I envision them, will provide both training and self-selection opportunities for prospective leaders. They were first developed during World War II by the U.S. Office of Strategic Services (OSS), whose mission was to send secret agents behind enemy lines. These agents had to be able to adjust to whatever conditions existed. (Does this sound like higher education?) Objective, systematic means of identifying candidates were developed. Differences among the candidates on such variables as energy and initiative, intelligence, social relations, leadership, and the like were determined through the use of a variety of testing mechanisms including conventional measures of intellectual ability, psychiatric interviews, physical toughness tests, and numerous real-world problems.

Since that time, many organizations throughout the world have been using similar methods, mostly for executive selection. AT&T was one of the pioneers in this effort and other Fortune 500 firms have utilized the concepts for similar purposes.

Participants in assessment centers take part in a number of exercises, usually four to seven, which last anywhere from one half-day to several weeks. Typical activities include the following:

- In-basket exercises
- Leaderless group discussions
- Role playing
- Case analysis
- In-depth interviews
- Management or simulation games
- Psychological and/or mental ability testing

Those who continue to use this method have found it successful, both in selection and in personal and career development. A number of research studies show that assessments can be reliable and—if done properly— valid.[1]

This activity could be adapted to higher education—as a part of the Diamond project—or any other activity that supports the development of leaders. Of course it would take time to identify the skill areas, to develop the assessments, and to train a group of people to administer the tests and to provide the evaluations.

The assessments might look like the following examples:

- In-basket exercise. A typical day in the life of the president, senior administrator, or dean is represented by a full in-basket. The participant is instructed to go through the contents of the in-basket, prioritize, solve problems, answer questions, delegate, orga-

APPENDIX A

Y ou will find here a collection of my regular newsletters, *BuzzWords*. These are one-page communications that give me an opportunity to express my views and to stimulate reaction from the university community. Topics aside, this is an effective, low-key method of keeping in touch with that critical internal audience as well as beyond, thanks to the Internet. It's also been a vehicle to help people keep on track as the institution continually evolves and improves.

BUZZWORDS

| Thoughts on SUIQ from | Chancellor Kenneth A. Shaw |

This fall the University hosted its annual Fall Friday receptions for prospective students and parents. Nothing unusual about that. It's something we've been doing here for more than 20 years.

But this year we entertained a record number of people. During the Veteran's Day holiday alone, we had 1,700 visitors. And even though the campus was more crowded than usual, operations ran so smoothly that disruptions were minimal and the mood was pleasant.

To me, there were two things worth noting about these occasions. First, it appears from the sheer volume of interest that the good word about Syracuse University is spreading. And second, the staff is very good at what it does.

We can all take credit for the first phenomenon because of the second observation: we are getting better at delivering the services to students (prospective and otherwise) and parents want and need. In part, that is because there is such a thing as SUIQ.

While I am certainly gratified by what I have observed as SUIQ has developed and taken hold on this campus, I'm not really surprised. I knew when I arrived here four and a half years ago that Syracuse University was ripe for this kind of initiative. So many factors that support a quality improvement initiative were already in place.

First, the staff included hundreds of talented and motivated people. Among this group, the great majority had a long term commitment to the institution. They knew Syracuse University, its history and traditions, its students and alumni, and its weaknesses and strengths. These were people ready and willing to improve the quality of the work they came here each day to do.

Second, this was an institution accustomed to change. Throughout its 125 years it adjusted to economic crises like the Great Depression, opened its doors to thousands of returning veterans after World War II, developed new programs to serve a changing student body and a changing world, and reached outward with study abroad opportunities and international student enrollment. It was ready to deal with the demographic and economic changes the 1990s ushered in.

In short, I don't think there could have been an environment more conducive to quality improvement than Syracuse in 1992. As most of us remember, we adopted a step-by-step approach to introducing SUIQ, beginning with the pilot teams of 1992-93 and continuing with the training of our 3,000 staff members now in process and expected to be complete by June 1996.

Back to the Beginning

Of course, we haven't waited until all the training is complete before we "do quality." Evidence, including the great Fall Fridays I mentioned, is all around us. In fact, I like to think that people here have been improving continuously since 1870; it's just that SUIQ has made it easier and faster to do.

I'll be talking about some of those successes and other topics related to SUIQ in future issues of *BuzzWords*. In the meantime, I'll leave you with the simple philosophy that drives quality improvement at Syracuse University:

1. We understand that service requires a team effort.
2. We serve everyone who comes to us for help; if we don't know the answer, we find someone who does.
3. Policies and procedures can be explained simply. If they can't, they must be rewritten or discarded.
4. We simplify our own procedures rather than create new layers of bureaucracy to deal with problems.
5. We note those problems we see out of our own areas to that they can be solved or simplified.

BUZZWORDS

Thoughts on SUIQ from

Chancellor Kenneth A. Shaw

SUIQ is based on the belief that quality improvement is possible only in an environment where openness and candor are not only encouraged but expected.

That's a well-founded belief and also a matter of common sense. It's not that improvement can't happen if changes flow only from the top down. It can. But lasting improvement comes when ideas are generated at every level and from everyone associated with the work that must get done.

On this campus, SUIQ works because problem solving is the job of the corrective action teams that rely on members' skills, not their places in the hierarchy. The snow-removal improvements you read about in the Jan. 22 SUIQ Report in the Syracuse Record would have been less successful if the people who actually operate the plows and maintain the buildings hadn't participated and had their suggestions acted on.

In my view, reluctance to address problems or fear of speaking one's mind are major barriers to progress. The more we can eliminate them, the faster we move toward achieving our vision as the nation's leading student-centered research university. That, by the way, is a place that is not only very good for students; it is also a great place to work.

Now, there is a very real difference between honest discussion and wallowing in negativity. One way to guarantee that only unproductive wheel-spinning happens is to play a game called "Ain't It Awful!" That happens when people try to top each other's tale of woe until it seems there is no way out. Self-pity and cynicism are also sure-fire barriers to progress. So is blaming people, rather than examining processes to see what can be changed.

I believe the best way to ensure that teamwork can actually bring about positive change is to be positive from the beginning. Believing that something can be done, even if the change is small,

Unafraid Plain Talk

stimulates creative thinking. A "glass half full" attitude can be contagious, leading others to want to join in and share their ideas. That's what can lead to productive brainstorming and creative solutions.

SUIQ training sessions dealt with elements of constructive group discussions. In Course II, we learned that interpersonal behaviors can stimulate or stifle active participation. When people act aggressively in a group, they tend to dominate by being rigid or by putting others down. When they act non-assertively, they are unwilling to address concerns and prefer to go along with what they think the leader wants. Assertive people, however, concentrate on progress by listening to others, giving their own ideas, and focusing on the issue at hand.

In that course, we also heard about the best way to conduct a brainstorming session. The principle rules are:

• Rule out criticism—ideas will be judged later.

• Welcome free-wheeling—the wilder the suggestions, the better.

• Strive for quantity—the greater the number, the greater the likelihood of finding a winner.

• Look for combinations—two ideas together can be one, much better idea.

• Have group members participate in sequence—that encourages everyone to join in, even if they choose to pass at first.

• Let ideas percolate for a while—then pick the one that rises to the top almost of its own accord.

You'll know when your session was a good one when everyone feels a part of the action, when people arrive and leave with a sense of purpose, and when all participants feel they have been heard. These outcomes are possible only when unafraid plain talk is the rule.

Once people feel comfortable with speaking their minds in a constructive way, good teamwork will happen. That's the topic of the next *BuzzWords*.

BUZZWORDS

Thoughts on SU**IQ** from   Chancellor Kenneth A. Shaw

Judging from the feedback I've been getting about SUIQ, there is more teamwork going on across campus than ever before. As the February 26 SUIQ Report in the *Syracuse Record* noted, there are more than 40 teams (QITs or CATS) in place in Student Affairs alone. Odds are, then, that you are a team member right now or soon will be.

Some of you may approach this assignment with some trepidation because similar experiences have been frustrating. There is a grain of truth in the old saying, "A camel is a horse made by a committee."

However, I am convinced that teams can work. And I know that SUIQ's success depends on good teamwork. This is the best way to draw from members' expertise in order to create better processes. A team's efforts are also far more likely to earn acceptance than an edict from top management.

So, how do effective teams work?

Good teams have a **well-defined mission**. They know what their goals are and can proceed to define the steps needed to reach them. They know how to determine when success has been achieved. For example, an Admissions Office Corrective Action Team's mission might be to answer inquiries from prospective students within 24 hours. The goal and the measurement criteria are clearly imbedded in the mission, and all team members know exactly what they are to accomplish.

Effective teams are made up of people who support the mission. Members need to believe that their task has value and that achieving their goals will make a real difference to the institution and the people it serves. In the case above, responding to inquiries within one day can be seen as important to future students and vital to a student-centered research institution like this one.

Teams must be willing to **commit time and energy to achieve the mission**. Once people who have a stake in the process come together, they need to spend time, gather information, discuss all aspects of the issue, and come to consensus. This is seldom a speedy process, and those who expect a quick fix will be disappointed.

Once these steps have been accomplished, team members must practice effective group skills and be-

Working in Teams

haviors. Some of these, such as brainstorming and assertiveness, were identified in the last *BuzzWords*.

To me, though, the most critical group skill is listening. Simple though it may seem, good listening is something very few people do consistently. Too often, we compose our own response while someone is talking or make judgments about the person and the idea instead of focusing on what's actually being said.

Good listeners:

• **Give the speaker plenty of time to talk.** They avoid interruptions, except to ask pertinent questions, and understand the value of silence and attention as aids to discussion.

• **Feed back to the speaker what has been said.** Good listeners can paraphrase a message to increase understanding and move discussions forward.

• **Indicate areas of agreement and disagreement.** By letting the speaker know the areas of harmony, good listeners not only set a positive tone, they eliminate areas that need no further discussion. Areas of disagreement become the focus as problems to be solved or barriers to overcome.

Other skills are important to good teamwork. It is essential to **stay on track** for example. While some socializing is to be expected and welcomed at the beginning of any meeting, staying on target by avoiding outside issues is essential to make best use of everyone's valuable time.

It's also important to **encourage every member of the team to participate.** Team members can jumpstart their silent colleagues by asking questions that require more than a yes or no response. Consensus and ownership of the process is far more likely to occur when everyone has had a say in the results.

If teams follow these guidelines most of the time, I believe they will discover they can be far more effective. This is not to say that every group experience will be easy and trouble-free. Conflict is inevitable whenever two or more people work together.

But I don't believe conflict is a bad thing, nor should it be avoided. Conflict resolution is possible, and that will be the topic of the next *BuzzWords*.

BUZZWORDS

Thoughts on SU**IQ** from   Chancellor Kenneth A. Shaw

I t's unfortunate that the word "conflict" stirs up negative reactions. Many people equate the term with fighting, loud voices, and hurt feelings. In reality, though, conflict is simply a difference of opinions and is inevitable in any setting where two or more people work together.

Conflict can also be a catalyst for constructive change if we learn to manage it. There are some proven tools to use while maintaining an attitude that differences can be resolved—if not to everyone's satisfaction, then for the benefit of the entire team.

Social scientists and psychologists have studied conflict management in great detail. I won't attempt to describe all the theories and guidelines that have enjoyed favor over the decades. There are, though, three models that I find useful.

The **Collegial Model** describes a process in which experts discuss the best way to accomplish a goal and come to a conclusion far better than any of the participants could have managed on their own. This requires that each person contribute ideas and suggestions for the common good and that everyone embrace the wisdom of the group in the end. That's a nice idea, but on that is very difficult to achieve.

That's because each person comes to the table with unique personal needs, perspectives, and prejudices. True conflict resolution must take these human characteristics into account, allow them to be aired, and incorporate them into the process. The perfect solution—100 percent acceptable to all and foolproof—is a laudable goal but we must remain realistic.

The **Zero Sum Model** describes win/lose scenario. As in a game of chess or football someone or some team will have to lose everything. Those who play this kind of conflict management game are out to win, no matter the cost, even if the solutions are bad ones. Fortunately, this model too, is rarely seen in the real world.

The **Strategic Negotiations Model** is what we usually follow in this country. Each side in this form of conflict management finds it advantageous to yield some of its demands in order to reach consensus.

Consensus, by the way, is a feeling, not an actual state of being. It is there when the group becomes willing to adopt one of several options available, even

Managing Conflict

though some individuals may have mild reservations about the outcome. Hard to define, consensus is readily apparent when it happens.

Reaching this point is made easier if we use some time-tested techniques.

First, **listen.** Try to suspend judgment for the time being. Make eye contact with the speaker to show you are paying close attention. Allow the time necessary to present a point. Use this opportunity to gather all the information you can.

Second, give the speaker feedback about what you have heard. This isn't always easy to do, since we tend to jump ahead to giving our own opinions. Remember, **feedback** is not agreeing or disagreeing, criticizing or blaming, diagnosing, praising, ordering, threatening, moralizing, giving advice, asking questions, or problem solving. Rather, feedback is a simple restatement of what the speaker has said, at least from your perspective. This will give him or her time to clarify a point or add more information. Just as important, feedback is a clear sign did you have, in fact, been listening.

State areas of agreement. Even the most contentious situations have some common ground, though it may be as basic as wanting coffee available at meetings. Most times, there are many areas where parties see eye to eye. Pointing these out helps participants think positively about the possibility of solutions.

Isolate areas of disagreement. If the other three steps have been followed, coming to the *"nub"* of the problem will seem far less threatening than would be the case if the meeting had begun with these issues. Now it is far more likely that participants will focus constructively on the work that must be done to reach consensus.

This is not to say that managing conflict will always be a swift and smooth process. Some problems have deep roots and a long history of contention and negative associations. Sometimes weeks and months of discussions must take place before there is any progress.

Nevertheless, the techniques I have described do work. I have seen them move mountains of problems, allowing participants to move forward to the greater improvements and increasing quality that make coming to work each day worthwhile.

BUZZWORDS

Thoughts on SU**IQ** from   Chancellor Kenneth A. Shaw

It's said that universities are places where the first law is "Nothing should be done for the first time." There are days when that seems to be the case.

However, change does happen on university campuses. We've seen that here at Syracuse. Downsizing has led to layoffs, for example, leaving other employees to miss their colleagues and often take on more work as well. On a more positive note, SUIQ has ushered in greater teamwork and more shared responsibility.

No matter what, though, change always causes stress. Even positive changes can be very disruptive. Babies, for example, are almost always a source of joy, but they certainly do require a great deal of new behavior from their parents. A promotion on the job is a reason for celebration, but adjusting to the new demands often takes six months or longer.

It's no wonder that most of us have resisted change at one time or another. Until we are comfortable with the new, we are unsure, even frightened, about our ability to adapt and adjust. Fear is often expressed as negativity or as a wish to go back to the old ways.

I think a great deal is accomplished once we accept that change is hard. But there are other tips for managing the process that have proved to be helpful.

1. Make sure the purpose of the change is clear and easy to understand. It should be possible for everyone involved to state that purpose and explain it to others.

2. Keep lines of communication open. With access to information and an opportunity to discuss and offer suggestions, we are all more likely to feel comfortable with changes as they happen.

3. Involve everyone affected by the change in the process whenever possible. Top-down decisions may seem easier to make, but they are far more likely to be resisted by those who feel left out or ignored.

4. Allow extra time for training, staff development, seminars, or conferences. Staff retreats are sometimes helpful, as are training sessions led by outside experts. Here at SU, the quality improvement initiative

Managing Change

has been guided through comprehensive training sessions. These, too, have changed over time in response to staff members' suggestions.

5. Provide constant feedback and reassurance that progress is being made. Open communication goes a long way toward accomplishing this goal. But more formal procedures such as department newsletters, bulletin boards—the cork variety as well as the electronic kind—and frequent team meetings can serve as effective ways to measure progress and keep all concerned on track.

6. Expect conflict and manage, rather than suppress, it. No change was ever implemented without some friction. Sometimes all that's needed is a safe forum where feelings can be expressed. (Principles for effective conflict management appeared in the March '96 edition *of BuzzWords.*)

7. Make use of recognition and incentives whenever possible. The Chancellor's Fund for Innovation was helpful here to support new ideas for the classroom. Recognition for significant successes through SUIQ as well as milestone achievements is now built in to the Syracuse Record. More efforts along these lines are forthcoming.

8. Respect the past. Acknowledging the contributions of the past allows people to preserve a sense of history and connection while slowly accommodating to new processes.

9. Move cautiously and succeed rather than swiftly and fail. Too many good ideas have died on the vine because the implementers demanded all or nothing. If a new process can be introduced in stages or adopted on an experimental basis, it has a far better chance to win approval and be effective in the long run.

I think we all know that any living thing, including a dynamic university like this one, is always changing. That doesn't mean a smooth and painless process, though. Change can be made easier if we pay attention to the essential ingredients—the people who will make this a better place to learn and work.

BUZZWORDS

Thoughts on SUIQ from   Chancellor Kenneth A. Shaw

O ver the course of the past year or so, I've heard some staff and administrators wonder aloud how SUIQ can succeed when a supervisor doesn't believe in focusing on the customer, rejects new ideas almost immediately, manages by intimidation, and, in short, just doesn't get it. That's a very legitimate question, especially since SUIQ training is designed to support and enhance team work, not autocratic, top-down management.

It is frustrating to watch other areas and departments move more swiftly toward the team approach that is at the heart of SUIQ. That is doubly so when personalities appear to be the cause of the problem. With due respect to the fact that change often takes more time at a university than at a corporation, problems do need to be addressed as they arise.

So what do employees do when they believe their supervisor is a bottleneck to progress?

1. Don't give up — The worst thing you can do is sit back, resigned to the idea that change is impossible. In fact, that's the easy way out. People with ideas always run the risk of criticism and rejection. They persevere anyway because they care about the work they do and about the institution they serve.

2. Meet with your boss for an honest discussion — If you perceive a problem, talk about it. You can do this without blaming, complaining, or getting too personal. Concentrate on your desire to deliver the best quality work you can offer. Provide specifics about the barriers to progress you have observed. Be prepared for differing views from your supervisor and for the possibility that you have misperceived the source of the problem when in fact it comes from somewhere else in the University.

3. Take another look at your suggestions — If your ideas have been rejected, find out why. Consider the input you get from your boss and make adjustments in your proposal if you think they are warranted. Or you could try your idea out with trusted colleagues for more input. Assuming you are still convinced your idea is worthwhile, you might consider going to the Quality Council or Quality Improvement Team for your area for another hearing.

Human Barriers to Progress

4. Think about the timing of your idea—If, in spite of a fair hearing, your idea is still rejected, it may be the timing of your suggestions is out of sync. There may be too much going on already in your area or it may be a particularly busy time of the year. Put your thoughts on paper and file them away for another time. It could turn out that your idea is not really a good one. But it might give rise to another good suggestion that could be adopted more readily.

All that said, it may well be that your supervisor really is the obstacle to change. If that is so your unit's lack of progress or inability to meet customers' needs is much more likely to be observed in an environment where continuous improvement is the norm. If other areas are making gains, then your area's inability to get with the program will stand out.

I believe that the performance evaluation process is also helpful in isolating problems. When I evaluate my cabinet officers, I seek input not only from their peers but also from those who report to them or interact with them regularly. Of course, I maintain strict confidentiality so that respondents can express their feelings honestly. As this method is modeled across the University, those supervisors who continue to obstruct progress will be identified and guided toward greater effectiveness.

Proponents and scholars of the continuous improvement method, often known as total quality management or TQM, maintain that barriers to change are very rarely attributable to personalities. While they acknowledge that progress may be quite slow, these experts demonstrate through study after study that TQM can galvanize organizations to new levels of excellence.

That is not to say that people in management positions are never the problem. Sometimes supervisors are simply too threatened by change and stand in the way of progress. They need to be identified and either guided to the new approaches or asked to find another work environment. Or, to put it in the vernacular, either move on or move off!

BUZZWORDS

Thoughts on SU**IQ** from   Chancellor Kenneth A. Shaw

If there is one consistent concern about the implementation of SUIQ here, it has been the omission of faculty from the training process. The great majority of staff members believe they have benefited from SUIQ, but some wonder why professors are not mandated to training as they have been. Some professors have wondered why they have not been included.

I've heard a few creative, though quite wrong, explanations for this phenomenon. First, it's said that faculty don't need to be concerned with serving others. Not so. While the teaching/learning process is, of course, different from filling a printing order or designing a departmental computer system, it certainly does involve anticipating students' needs and meeting them through effective advising, prompt return of papers and tests, fair grading, and so on.

A second supposition is that faculty have no need of the interpersonal and group skills taught in SUIQ training, nor do they need to understand the steps staff members are taking to improve their own work. Not true. Everyone can use some more training in interpersonal communication. And faculty do need to know about the training process and the efforts underway through the quality improvement teams and corrective action teams all across campus. But providing this kind of information doesn't require a full-scale training program such as the one staff have participated in.

There are valid reasons for not mandating SUIQ training for faculty. Their work requires a different approach to improve its quality. The focus is on the promotion of learning, and, therefore, the process for improvement rests primarily with the individual professor and the courses she or he teaches.

The basic principles in this case are as follows:

1. Develop learning outcomes or goals for students in each course.

Faculty and SUIQ

2. Provide the experiences that will move students toward these goals.

3. Measure student progress toward the goals.

4. Make adjustments as necessary to improve the course the next time.

There is clear evidence that this is happening as faculty clarify and refine their expectations for students in their courses and as they use increasingly more diverse methods to help students achieve these goals.

There is, of course, much more to be done. At both the course and program levels, there needs to be greater concentration on defining the desired learning outcomes, designing and providing the necessary learning experiences that will bring about those outcomes, evaluating progress, and adjusting as necessary. In higher education, this is known as outcomes assessment, a very complex but essential process.

Assessment for the broader SUIQ program is guided by surveys of students, staff, and alumni, which have and improved of late. For faculty efforts, though, the picture is not nearly as clear. In addition to traditional measures such as faculty publications, accreditation, and faculty/student ratios, we need to expand such initiatives as student portfolios, senior theses, and general competency tests. At the same time, we must continue to search for new evaluation methods and copy the best practices of other higher education institutions.

Faculty will continue to learn about SUIQ through campus-wide publications such as the Record, through departmental newsletters, and other communications. The most important illustration of this initiative comes from the genuine successes that staff have posted through their work and from the growing satisfaction of external and internal customers.

BUZZWORDS

Thoughts on SUIQ from   Chancellor Kenneth A. Shaw

On Civility

What does it cost to practice civility in our lives? What do we sacrifice when we respond politely to a question, give our full attention to someone with a problem, or let someone ahead in line?

If you go by what passes for human interaction these days, the price is evidently too high. You know that if you wait at a store counter while the clerk finishes a personal phone call in front of you or if you get the distinct impression that your requests are inconveniencing the "customer service" representative. You know it when you get cut off in traffic or when your enjoyment of a movie is ruined by loud conversations taking place behind you in the theater.

The problem is exacerbated, in my mind, by the "entertainment" available in the media. Talk shows feature physical confrontation at worst and outright rudeness at best. Even on such established programs as the *Today Show,* guests talk over each other and the interviewer, shedding no light on the subject at hand. And sit-coms offer situations in which sarcasm and put-downs are the main sources of humor.

Admittedly, the subject of civility is getting some ink these days. But it's easy to talk about the lack of courtesy in everyday life. Who doesn't support politeness, good manners, and tact?

Syracuse University is fortunate to have a staff and faculty that practices the art of civility daily. The great majority of the people here are polite by nature and have demonstrated again and again a commitment to students and to each other that is above and beyond the call of duty. Very often this commitment plays out under great stress, a sign of genuine courtesy.

I don't mean to imply that civility can take place only in the absence of conflict. Conflict is an inevitable and even welcome part of the life of any university since it is a critical catalyst for learning and growth. Nevertheless, exercising respect for another's views even while disagreeing is the soul of civil behavior.

Neither do I mean we must accept abusive behavior from others or sit quietly in the face of socially destructive attitudes such as racism and sexism. This is a community united in the search for truths, and we are duty bound to expose ideas that have no basis in fact.

The SUIQ training program is intertwined with lessons in civility. The assertiveness, active listening, and encouragement of creative thinking taught as essential group skills are really just excellent workplace etiquette. When we can present our ideas without intimidating others, work toward better understanding, and support each other's ideas for improving the work we do together, we are being civil in the best possible way.

There's another word that comes to mind: respect. To my mind, it means seeing value in every person with whom we interact and respecting that value with our words and actions. Thus we can accept another's perspective even while holding a contradictory idea.

There are some solid practical reasons for increasing the civility factor on campus. First, behaving respectfully to one another goes a long way toward reducing unnecessary stress and strain in the work day. Second, by practicing good workplace manners, we demonstrate to students that the escalation of disrespect out in the world today isn't the norm for educated people.

Finally, civility is a essential ingredient in our core values of quality, diversity, innovation, service, and caring — especially the last.

BUZZWORDS

Thoughts on SU**IQ** from   Chancellor Kenneth A. Shaw

Ask a prospective student what she remembered most about her visit to Syracuse University and chances are you won't hear: "I was relieved to know it meets all the requirements for the Middle States Accreditation review."

What you might hear—and I certainly hope you *do* hear—is that the campus was well tended, the people were friendly and helpful, and the students were both interested and interesting. Ask for more information and you could learn that the staff and faculty this prospect met were quick to respond to questions and, if they didn't have an answer, found someone who did. In short, this prospective student came away from her visit with the strong impression that people cared about her and it showed.

From what I observe, this kind of impression is the rule rather than the exception here at an Syracuse University. Whether they know it or not, staff and faculty who convey a good feeling to future and current students are being customer focused.

There's that word. Customer. It's a term that many say doesn't fit the academic environment. After all, the University is not a hardware store or a car dealership. The admissions office doesn't work on commission, professors aren't paid according to students' assessment of their performance, and nobody tips the staff from the physical plant for a walk well shoveled.

Nor do we aim, as some manufacturing concerns do, to achieve "zero defects." Our products are educated citizens who are, of course, human beings with all the natural imperfections of the species.

We can, however, set continuous improvement as a goal and use SUIQ as a method to achieve it. Making it possible to work smarter in a very competitive higher education market is the basic reason SUIQ exists. We know that if we don't increase the number of satisfied customers, another institution will.

Customer Is an 8-Letter Word

But even the most earnest resolve won't cause continuous improvement unless we know what needs improving. And that leads us back to the customers again. They need to be able to tell us what they need. Not what we *think* they need, but what they need.

Finding out, then, is the first step. The basis for this part of the process is rooted in the social sciences, where we've learned that information is often best sought in the field directly from the subjects themselves.

It's a bottom-up mentality, and it requires being able to really listen. Of course, that's the same kind of thinking that guides SUIQ. We "listen" to our students primarily through surveys at the area or department levels and through campus-wide surveys such as the one for graduating seniors.

They've told us what they find helpful and what they see as a hassle. Having a registration canceled because of a financial hold, for example, is in the major hassle category. So every semester, the Bursar's Office tries to beat its record-low numbers from the time before. Now it's not a stretch to imagine that problems like this will virtually disappear.

This story can be repeated in countless ways all over this campus. And it all stems from listening to the customer, making adjustments, implementing those adjustments, and asking the customer again for his feedback.

Now, does this mean the customer is always right? No. Not even the most service-oriented business today would agree with that. That's why I've concentrated on customer needs rather than customer wants. There's a difference, one that is especially clear in an academic setting.

That will be the subject of the next *BuzzWords*.

BUZZWORDS

Thoughts on SU**IQ** from   Chancellor Kenneth A. Shaw

Operating from a customer focus is the heart and soul of any attempt to improve quality. That's what everyone involved in the total quality management effort stresses. It's the point I made in the last edition of *BuzzWords*.

Here at SU, we've made good progress in this direction. The evidence is in such innovations as the grades-by-phone system, access to personal financial information by computer, extended hours in the computer clusters, and smaller classes for all new students. For faculty and staff, work is underway to increase workplace satisfaction in response to the information gathered by focus groups in the fall of 1995. One significant improvement — an all-University recognition program — will be implemented in the fall.

Nevertheless, there are limits to meeting customer's perceived needs. McDonald's is a good example. They do an excellent job of meeting customer orders from a limited menu. But try to order prime rib there, and you'll be frustrated. They don't serve it and they won't try, even if you protest that you are, in fact, their customer.

The difference between wants and needs is even more evident on college campuses. Students come to here learn under faculty guidance, just as they did in medieval times when learned people gathered to share ideas and to impart knowledge to those who wished to learn from them. The faculty came first, in other words, and the students second.

And the faculty has remained in charge of the learning process in the centuries since. They set the curriculum, assess student performance, and certify the degree of learning that has taken place by providing grades. Student evaluations of faculty performance do matter, of course, but even then the faculty

Who's in Charge Here?

determine what is truly important. For example, I recall a professor at another university whose students continually marked him down for his eccentric wardrobe and gruff demeanor. Nevertheless, they praised his ability as a teacher. That, to me, was evidence that the students were getting what they needed but not everything they wanted.

Today universities exist primarily to help undergraduate students grow intellectually and socially. To do that we provide an environment conducive to that growth including safe residence halls, healthy food, a variety of counseling choices, and other supportive services. We also provide rigorous intellectual pursuits to be experienced in and out of the classroom under faculty supervision.

We do not, however, provide everything students tell us they want. In fact, sometimes we make getting what they need difficult for them. For example, experience shows us that ambiguity and conflict of ideas create the tension necessary to promote active learning. Good teaching often means withholding "the answers" in favor of encouraging students to seek information on their own. We also know that making learning too easy means that not much learning of value will take place.

Similarly, if we were able to meet every staff request, salaries would be much higher and parking would be free. Here the limitations are financial. As our restructuring process has taught us, budgets are finite and trade-offs necessary in order to maintain and improve the quality of our collective mission as a university.

Our customers are key to SUIQ. From them we learn what's working and what needs to change. The emphasis is always on the need.

BUZZWORDS

Thoughts on SU**IQ** from   Chancellor Kenneth A. Shaw

Hope springs eternal in the fall on a college campus. Students, faculty, and staff feel renewed, charged up, and ready to change what needs to be changed to do things right this time.

But then comes the rush of projects, deadlines, papers to be graded, and meetings to attend , and we often find ourselves slipping into the rut of routine.

There is no question that change is difficult. Ask anyone who's trying to stick to a new exercise schedule or quitting smoking. In spite of the promised benefits of change, it's hard to let go of the familiar in favor of the new.

Nevertheless, it is by changing, adapting, and adjusting that people and the organizations they serve get better. I had an opportunity to observe this phenomenon in action not too long ago when I visited the re-engineered Barclay Law Library.

Over the last several years, it has transformed itself into a resource worthy of the fine faculty and students in the College of Law both now and in the future.

Change there involved reallocation of resources and prioritizing faculty and student needs. For example, a law library staff member was transferred from behind-the-scenes cataloging to direct contact with library users in need of assistance with technology. The result was better service and no undue delays in cataloging new acquisitions. Through surveys, the library determined that the essential Lexis/Nexis and WESTLAW databases could exist in electronic form only, eliminating the need for costly and space-consuming paper copies.

Real Change

I was impressed not only with the obvious improvements, but also with the hours of work and tolerance for frustration that was required of the staff, administrators, faculty, and students to make this "new" library work.

More than better information resource management emerged from these changes. Certain principles also became clear as the work to improve moved forward.

- Everyone's job needs to change.
- Everyone must acquire new technology skills and management strategies as work roles change.
- Staff and budget resources must be drawn from re-allocation requiring the tough decisions about priorities.
- Some old tasks must be eliminated in favor of those that come from the changes implemented.
- Measures of success must be based on the level of user satisfaction.

All of us are challenged by changes in the works. One of the most obvious is in our shifting computing infrastructure as mainframes give way to client server approaches. In time, we can expect big improvements in the way we seek and share information with each other. On the way, though, we can also expect the frustration and misgivings that any major change brings.

I'll have more to say about the principles listed above in future *BuzzWords*.

B U Z Z W O R D S

| Thoughts on SUIQ from | Chancellor Kenneth A. Shaw |

"The timing isn't quite right. Let's hold off for about six months."

"Let me know how your area is progressing. Maybe we can get together to talk about it sometime soon."

"Sure, we'd love to change the way we do things. Just give us some more money."

"If it ain't broke, don't fix it."

It's amazing what the human mind can do to itself in order to avoid change. And it's not just the individual who practices denial. Whole teams – even departments – can play the ostrich head-in-the-sand game in a variety of creative ways.

Resistance to new methods, technologies, and management can be expected initially. Foot dragging can be tolerated, at least for a while. Eventually, though, the time comes to take steps toward achieving real change.

The personal computer on my desk was not an entirely welcome addition at first. While I admired my colleagues who could make those machines do extraordinary things for them and while I believed them when they told me how essential computers would be in the future, I didn't want one.

Frankly, I was apprehensive. I wondered whether I could ever figure out how to really use one. I was concerned I might break the machine, causing gales of laughter to roll out of the computing support office.

But I did learn. I took advantage of the training and support that was offered, and I asked for help when I needed it. I spent time exploring the computer's capabilities on my own whenever I could. Now I'm not only computer savvy, I can surf the Net just like my grandchildren.

There's no question that using a computer has changed the way I work, just as it has for the great majority of us at the University. And that's just one

Ready or Not: Here Comes Change

of many changes, technological and otherwise, happening all over campus.

We are challenged to not only accommodate the current changes, but also to maintain the pace of change by continuously updating our skills and understanding. That way we're not only ready for the next change to come along, we become more flexible and adaptive in general. Like any skill, the art of change can be practiced.

The shift to the new client-server computing environment is a case in point. By permitting people to share information very quickly, this change will make it possible to streamline significantly many of our processes. For example, registering, dropping, and adding courses – already vastly improved over the days of eternal lines and waits – may soon require just one step.

For our students, this will be a major improvement. And for the University, this will be a big step in our ongoing quest to meet customer needs.

But it won't be without some stress and strain. There is the matter of acquiring new skills, of course. Building trust in the new system is another. It's natural for people to be suspicious of a change that relies on a machine to complete important tasks. (Banks find, for example, that people are quite happy to use ATMs for withdrawing cash. But most of us prefer depositing checks with a living, breathing teller rather than sending our hard earned funds into the bowels of a machine.)

Change is coming, like it or not. How we adapt to it – and help each other adapt – is within our control. Syracuse University means to be a place where change happens smoothly by helping its faculty and staff become better prepared.

That's why this phase of the SUIQ effort is dedicated to training and development and why each member of this community will be asked to dedicate at least one percent of working time to learning.

BUZZWORDS

Thoughts on SUIQ from   Chancellor Kenneth A. Shaw

S ummer is a quieter time on campus – but not, as some outside suspect, a state of suspended animation. There has always been a great deal of activity at Syracuse ranging from sports camps to institutes to Reunion. And classes happen, of course, though even these take on a different, perhaps more relaxed feeling during the warmer months.

Summer is also a time to begin projects or evaluate current ones in a more focused fashion than is possible during the rest of the academic year. There are three this summer that have occupied my attention and about which I'd like to share my thoughts with you.

They are:

- The beautification and safety projects on the north campus,
- the results of our Middle States review this spring, and
- the status of our efforts to both raise new funds and distribute those we have received.

Summer Thoughts

I'll concentrate on the most visible of these in this issue – the site work taking place between the School of Management and the Newhouse School and between Newhouse and the Schine Student Center. In July, I'll talk about the Middle States report, and in August I'll offer my thoughts on the Commitment to Learning fundraising campaign.

As it was described in the June 1 edition of the Record, the construction work underway is a continuation of ongoing initiatives to both recapture and enhance our campus. This project began in 1994 when we officially took ownership of the former city streets that wind through our space. That was done, as many of you recall, to guard against injuries to pedestrians (largely students, faculty, and staff), incidents which happened all too frequently when general traffic was permitted through campus 24 hours a day.

It is not enough, however, to simply take possession of these streets and post guards to restrict traffic. We must make these passageways and spaces truly campus-like. And that requires narrowing the streets, adding brick walkways, and changing the landscaping throughout.

This work has been described to me as making our area truly people friendly. When we're done, the streets will be more like private driveways, making the statement to all who work and study at Syracuse that pedestrians have the absolute right of way and vehicles are permitted as needed.

The transformation of the one-block street section between University Place and Waverly Avenue is another important step in this direction. That project will radically change the grade of the landscape, provide walkways, seating and lighting, and, most important, create a more dramatic view toward our most recognizable building, the Hall of Languages.

To me, the two most important aspects of all this work are these. First, reclaiming the campus feel of the University says more emphatically that this is a unique environment. This is a place where people come to learn by relying on each other and on a myriad of resources rarely found outside a research university.

Second, the obvious fact that we tend to our environment, that we are more than a series of cinderblock buildings loosely linked in an urban area makes a strong impression on visitors. Time and again we hear from prospective students and their families as well as from faculty candidates that this is a beautiful place. The various architectural styles knit together by planned landscaping and pathways form a whole that says we care about Syracuse University, its people, and most of all about the work that goes on here every day.

BUZZWORDS

Thoughts on SU**IQ** from   Chancellor Kenneth A. Shaw

On the Campaign Trail

Unless you are actively involved in fund raising for the University, it's easy to forget there is a campaign going on. But, as Chancellor, I never lose sight of the Commitment to Learning campaign, and I'm happy to report that it's right on target at $230 million on its way to exceeding its target of $300 million by 2000.

The implications of a successful campaign for Syracuse University are clear. It's here that we find the resources necessary to move our vision to reality. As I've often said, a fine university becomes better by relying on three key factors: a vision for the future, an outstanding faculty and staff, and a reliable source of support. The first two we have in hand. The third is an ongoing quest.

This campaign has attracted several large gifts since it began in 1993. In fact, 47 of these are over $1 million and include such multimillion additions as the Ruth Meyer bequest of more than $11 million, the $3.2 million Setnor gift to name the music school and its auditorium, and the more than $2 million Digital Equipment gift to the Maxwell School, among others.

These gifts are impressive and most welcome, of course. But so, too, are the thousands of smaller contributions because, when added together, they support our vision and our values – Quality, Caring, Diversity, Innovation, and Service — in very direct ways.

The Ruth Meyer bequest is the most outstanding example of the link between support and our vision. The lion's share of the gift — $5.7 million – has been allocated to endowed scholarships. The University Library has been granted a $2 million endowment for the support of research and $1 million supports undergraduate research across all schools and colleges. Another $1 million supports the annual College of Arts and Sciences freshmen lecture which this fall will be given by the Pulitzer Prize winning Doris Kearns Goodwin. Grants of $500,000 each have gone to the Soling Program, the College of Arts and Sciences Innovation Learning Program, and the Michael O. Sawyer Chair in Constitutional Law. Other monies have gone to the College of Law and the Tracy Ferguson Student Athlete Fund.

Each allocated dollar, in other words, of Ruth Meyer's very generous bequest has been pressed into the support of our students in a direct way. So, too, have thousands of other gifts, small and large. (For an account of the most recent contributions and the efforts they will support, see the article in the Spring/Summer 1998 *Syracuse Magazine*.)

And, while all the giving during the Commitment to Learning campaign has served our vision as the nation's leading student-centered research university, the growth in our ability to provide scholarship support is the most heartening to me. Since the campaign began, we've added a full $39.2 million to our endowed scholarship fund, monies that reach our students in the most direct way.

Scholarships range from all-University grants to Chancellor's and Dean's scholarships to scholarships specific to a school or college or to a discipline or major. These are the gifts that truly make a university education possible for hundreds of our students.

But they do more. They enable the University to become more competitive with the better colleges and universities in the country in the quest to attract bright, talented, and dedicated students. These are the young men and women who raise the bar here by working harder and smarter and by challenging us to become even better as a higher education institution. They tend to persist through graduation, one of the true quality indicators for a university. And they succeed in the wider world, thereby enhancing the Syracuse University image.

And most of all, they improve the quality of Syracuse University, which is after all only as good as the educated citizens it produces.

So I keep close tabs on the current Commitment to Learning campaign and on all our fundraising efforts. They lead us to the kind of support we must have to make our vision real.

BUZZWORDS

Thoughts on SUIQ from   Chancellor Kenneth A. Shaw

I s freedom of speech, that treasured legacy of the First Amendment to the U.S. Constitution, seen differently on the college campus? Yes and no.

Of course the first amendment is honored in higher education just as it is in the rest of the country.

But there is also the practice of granting academic freedom to faculty members. This freedom is linked to the concept of tenure and provides an environment in which professors can teach, research, and publish without fear of being fired for their views.

Thus, university and college campuses have become places where ideas—no matter how controversial—can be expressed with perhaps greater freedom than in other organizations. Thus it is no surprise that, in higher education, debates can be very heated and protests very vigorous.

While energy and enthusiasm pro and con can often lead to new understandings, sometimes they don't. Sometimes controversy stifles thought. This is especially true when groups of people believe that the positions they profess are the only right and true ones and that anyone who disagrees should be silenced.

Controversial speakers often know this. Not interested in debate, they have developed a repertoire of pat answers to the kinds of responses they tend to arouse. So engaging someone of this ilk can guarantee a contest to see who can be loudest or most outrageous.

The upshot is that the protest itself, both before and during the event, is the best kind of publicity for the speaker. It usually attracts attention from the media and places the spotlight on the very person the protesters claim to despise.

So what can those of us who value learning through discussion do under these circumstances? Below are my suggested alternatives:

• First, don't attend an event featuring speakers or groups with whom you sincerely disagree. That way you don't support the event with your

Freedom of Speech

presence. You will miss a chance to learn more, however. (This, to me, is the least desirable option.)

• Use all reasonable means—letters to the editor, teach-ins, and discussions—to communicate views counter to those of the speaker.

• Use the question and answer period after a speech to thoughtfully and reasonably point out any inaccuracies or inconsistencies in the presentation.

To me these are the alternatives most conducive to a learning environment. What's unacceptable is a wholesale effort to disrupt a speaker by shouting, chanting, and other means of harassment. That strategy is based on a belief that those with certain views do not deserve to be heard.

And, as a strategy, disruption is doomed to failure. First, it ascribes great power to the speaker's words. Neutral parties will naturally wonder what all the fuss is about and may even assume the speaker is right since there is no intelligent counter-argument in sight.

Second, speakers with experience can turn a disruption into a victory. Who has not seen a politician, for example, win the sympathy of the crowd by dealing effectively with hecklers?

Just as important, though, is the chilling effect that vocal harassment can have on a community like this one. If one speaker can be drowned out, then why not the next and the next? Disruption takes on a different meaning when it's directed at someone we wholeheartedly support.

Ultimately, this squelching behavior can lead to a place where only the most bland, centrist views can be aired.

As Chancellor, I'm frequently called upon to explain why we host certain speakers here. I'm pleased to respond that we believe that the pursuit of truth requires the presence of a vast array of ideas, no matter how controversial. Doing otherwise makes this something other than a university. Suppressing thought through disruption, however, poses a very real threat to both freedom of speech and to the ongoing pursuit of new knowledge.

APPENDIX B

Here you will find examples of the fame/shame syndrome that I've collected from some of my colleagues. (They had no trouble coming up with the incidents, but they begged me not to attribute them by name.) Then I suggest ways to keep your sanity intact...well, managed, at least. Leadership is serious business, to be sure. It is all-consuming but rewarding, especially on the good days. But good days can be few and far between, or maybe it just seems that way. One way to survive is to keep your sense of humor intact. I've always found that laughing at myself and at the situation was the best alternative to banging my head against the wall.

THE FAME/SHAME SYNDROME

"Sometimes you're the windshield, sometimes you're the bug," goes a song. And, though that's true for everyone, experiencing the highs and lows of leadership can feel more intense, especially when you occupy a highly visible position. A quick poll of some of my colleagues drew these examples of the fame/shame syndrome in action. (See my definition of the phenomenon in chapter 2.)

Never underestimate students' capacity for mayhem. One university president endured an hour-long phone call from an irate motel owner whose facility had been thoroughly trashed by the university rodeo club. Never mind that the motel was some distance from campus; the damage was definitely the president's fault. On the other hand, this same president was praised to the skies by a new grandmother who called to thank him profusely for the baby her son-in-law and faculty daughter had just produced. Though there was no possible connection (really!), the president remained gracious throughout the conversation.

A student art project livened the days of one colleague. The student had elected to extol the virtues of virginity in a very graphic way. With controversy spreading across the campus community, the president steadfastly defended the student's right to expression while at the same time using the example as an illustration of the social and political ramifications of exercising such a right. Hundreds of letters poured in, decrying this example of freedom of expression. Other writers, however, praised the president as a champion of the U.S. Constitution, defender of freedom of expression, and friend of the arts. On the other hand, she was once called to defend a student speaker's right to mention God in a commencement address. Once again, hundreds of letters came her way. Many excoriated her for her stand. Other writers, many of them deeply religious people, praised her.

Another higher education leader is frequently invited to bathe in the warm glow of reflected glory. His appointee to the position of vice president for research, for example, has won virtually every major award in his field. His children have gone on to exemplary careers in medicine and law. These achievements have been attributed to his skill as a mentor and parent, which he sees as only very loosely connected to the truth. On the other hand, when the football team, already suffering an ignominious season, was mired in the mud of a soggy stadium, that too was placed at the president's feet. As he says, "When the university's toilets back up, it's time to 'dis' the president."

Tangling with the athletics department is often a dicey process. One college president I know elected to trim the budget by appreciably cutting the number of slots on the football team. The hue and cry in opposition was deafening, with the primary accusation being that this leader was "ending football as we know it!" Three team members were dispatched to his office to plead the pro-football case, but the tactic backfired. "I'm not a tall person, but when I towered over these guys," said my colleague, "I felt as though I had saved them from certain injury by trimming the team." On the other hand, he reports a continuing stream of praise for the successful completion of a new library, a project that had begun long before his term of office.

SANITY MANAGEMENT

Leaders neglect their own mental health at their peril. I've seen far too many intelligent, sensitive, and committed people age 10 years in five, become cynical and bitter, and lose their sense of perspective because they couldn't or wouldn't take care of themselves. (Self-care is, by the way, your responsibility.)

Several techniques for cooling your jets exist. The tried and true activities include exercising, doing absolutely nothing, meditating, getting absorbed in a hobby, reading mystery novels, and visiting regularly with people who think you're wonderful—like your spouse, children, and grandchildren.

Leaders who ascend to more lofty perches, though, often need to do more. A colleague of mine very rarely entertains overnight guests in the university's official residence. That way he preserves his late evenings and early mornings for the reading and resting that are essential for his well-being. One leader I know has invested in a personal residence in another town that is never used for official university business. He doesn't have many opportunities to use this hideaway, but he takes comfort from the knowledge that it is always there.

Acting on the sure knowledge that physical exercise can make a big dent in stress levels, another colleague has installed a few pieces of exercise equipment plus a shower in her office. This way she can schedule a workout between the last appointment in the afternoon and the beginning of an evening engagement.

SOME DEFINITIONS

So often, words mean something far different from the dictionary definition. Certainly that is true in higher education where words can be elevated to the highest levels of obfuscation. Leaders must be prepared to see below the surface to the subtext. Here are some common terms and a sanitized version of what they really mean. While excessive cynicism can be destructive, a little lampooning is helpful—no, *essential*—to sanity management.

- Innovation: Something that has been tried elsewhere but that can now be passed off as new.
- Morale: A term that is nearly always accompanied by the phrase "is at an all-time low." It's good to know when this is really the case since the wise leader avoids a performance review at such times.
- View: Another term that is wedded to a phrase, in this case, "with alarm." It is used when someone's parking, classroom, or social space is under threat.
- Indecisive: Used when the leader won't make major cuts in someone else's budget.
- Unfeeling: Used when the leader makes major cuts in my budget.
- One of us: A phrase used to describe the new leader in his or her first six months to a year on the job. After that, it's, "She's a nice person but doesn't seem to have a clear agenda."
- Dictatorial: A label for a leader who made a decision without consulting me.
- Inclusive: The leader took my advice on an important issue over that of all those other people he consulted.

KNOWING WHEN TO LEAVE

Finally, it's important to know when to exit gracefully. You'll know that time has come when

- Students no longer have a quick response to the question, "What are the three things you like best about your university?"
- You change the subject when you are asked what you like best about your job.
- The faculty senate doesn't notice that you've missed three meetings in a row.
- You have to introduce yourself to students even though there are pictures of you in just about every institutional publication.
- Staff don't show up for recognition dinners.
- Your most loyal assistant avoids making eye contact with you.
- Your board provides a Yugo as your "company" car.
- You wake up to the realization that you have no plan.
- Your reputation is for defending your programs rather than creating new ones.

- You invite yourself to an alumni club meeting only to find it's been canceled for lack of interest.
- You sit down at an official function and no one rushes to fill the seat next to you.
- You feel tired all the time.
- You find yourself thinking that this would be a great place if there weren't all these students, faculty, and staff around.
- You don't feel the need to explain a controversial decision.
- You plan your vacations without looking at your campus and external obligations.
- You don't consult with others because you've begun to believe you always know what's best.
- Your key staff stop coming to you with important problems.
- You decide that your team has been together so long that performance reviews are no longer necessary.
- You forget to return the board president's call even after three insistent messages.
- You find you've spent the day with spinach caught between your front teeth and no one has thought to point it out to you.

A PARTING WORD

Okay, this is where I'll stop. That's not because I've run out of ideas about leadership. The topic is endlessly fascinating to me; I hope it is for you. Rather, this is a very brief primer on leadership, as promised in the preface. And like knowing when to leave, it's also important to know when to stop.

I hope you have found my thoughts useful. Some of you may have decided to stop before you start. If you believe that the shame would outpace the fame, that you can't make enough of a difference for leading to be worth the hard work and aggravation, or that your personal style and leadership of a higher education institution don't mesh, then declining the chance to lead is both legitimate and wise.

Others of you are now chomping at the bit to get started. For you, this book forms an outline of the competencies and skills you'll need to acquire and build on. There is much more that you'll need to do, of course, and why not begin now?

I wish you well. Good luck!

INDEX

by Kay Banning

Participation *(continued)*
  creativity and, 53
  leadership and, viii
Personal competence
  appearance and, 70
  emotional competence and, 14–17, 94
  personal inventory and, 56, 92, 96
  self-awareness and, 12–14, 21
  teams and, 65
Personal detachment, 61
Personal-related currencies, 37
Political leadership, 18
Position-related currencies, 36, 37
Power
  exercise of, 34–35, 92–93
  interpersonal competence and, 26, 27,
    31–35, 86
  leadership and, viii
  sources of, 32–34
The Power of the Presidency and Presidential Leadership (Fisher), 34
Press
  good news/bad news and, 90
  leadership and, viii
  position-related currencies and, 36
  public relations and, 70, 72–73
Principle of least group size, 44, 93
Problem definition, 62
Problem questions, and interview
  techniques, 65
Public relations
  fund-raising and, 69, 74
  ground rules of, 70–71
  press and, 70, 72–73
  public as constituency, 68
  realities of, 69–70
Public speaking. *See* Speeches
Purdue University, xiii

Quakers, 50
Quality improvement plans. *See also*
  Syracuse University Improving
  Quality (SUIQ)
  administrative units and, 5–6
  organizations and, 66–67
  restructuring and, 7, 66

Rational leadership, 18
Raven, B., 32

Reality, and emotional competence, 15
Relationship-related currencies, 37–38
Relaxation, 78–79, 94, 119
Repetition
  organizational grief and, 61
  values and, 10, 11
  of vision, 92
Respect, and motivation, 38–39
Restructuring
  change and, 7, 63
  conflict resolution and, 25
  guidelines for, 4–5
  organizational grief and, viii, 3–4, 5, 7,
    59
  quality improvement plans and, 7, 66
  of Syracuse University, vii, 1–8
Rewards
  change and, 58
  inspiration-related currencies and, 36
  motivation and, 35, 94
  organizational grief and, 61
  reward power, 32, 35
  teams and, 64

Self-awareness, 12–14, 21
Self-evaluation, 17
Self-love, 17, 94
Self-selection, 96, 99
Social distance, 33–34
Social exchange theory, 9
Social/emotional needs, 45, 46, 61
Society of Friends, 50
Southern Illinois University, xiii
Speakers
  freedom of speech and, 116
  public relations and, 69
Speeches
  ceremonial events and, 78
  fear of, 71–72
  honesty and, 4, 7
  leadership and, viii
  public relations and, 71–72
  restructuring and, 6
  Syracuse University Improving Quality
    and, 67
  35 percent rule and, 76–77
  values and, 4
Stability, 55
Staff
  budgets and, 79–80